21 Activities

MARK TWAIN

R. KENT RASMUSSEN

FOR KiDS

His Life & Times

W9-BNL-749

2/05

**LIBRARY OF CONGRESS
CATALOGING-IN-PUBLICATION DATA**

Rasmussen, R. Kent.
Mark Twain for kids : his life and times,
21 activities / R. Kent Rasmussen.
p. cm.
Includes bibliographical references and index.
ISBN 1-55652-527-3
1. Twain, Mark, 1835—1910—Juvenile literature.
2. Authors, American—19th century—Biography—
Juvenile literature. I. Title.
PS1331.R375 2004
8189.409—dc22   2004003529

COVER AND INTERIOR DESIGN: Monica Baziuk

INTERIOR PHOTOS AND ILLUSTRATIONS: pages v, 16, 30, 32, 33, 38, 40, 41, and 104 from *Life on the Mississippi,* 1883. Pages vi, x, 83, 90, 98, 127, 128, 129, 131, 132, and 138 courtesy of the Library of Congress. Pages xii and 116 courtesy of Barbara Schmidt. Pages xiii, 3, 7, and 108 from *Adventures of Huckleberry Finn,* 1884. Pages xiv and 6 courtesy of PhotoDisc. Pages 2, 5, 22, 25, 31, 42, 58, 74, 88, 89, 109, 117, 121, 126, and 137 from A. B. Paine, *Mark Twain: A Biography,* 1912. Pages 6, 8, 9, 13, 14, and 15 from *The Adventures of Tom Sawyer,* 1876. Pages 9, 75, 79, 80, and 81 from *The Innocents Abroad,* 1869. Pages 17, 24, 26, 37, 43, 44, 56, 127, 134, and 135 from A. B. Paine, "The Boys' Life of Mark Twain," *St. Nicholas* magazine, Oct. 1915–Oct. 1916. Pages 20, 52, 86, and 93 courtesy of the Mark Twain Project, The Bancroft Library. Page 27 from Donald Seitz, *Artemus Ward,* 1919. Pages 48, 50, 51, 53, 54, 57, 59, 60, 70, 72, and 73 from *Roughing It,* 1872. Pages 61, 68, 87, 99, and 106 courtesy of R. Kent Rasmussen. Pages 62 and 95 from *The Gilded Age,* 1874. Pages 64, 65, and 67 from *Sketches, Old & New,* 1875. Pages 66, 99, and 100 from *A Tramp Abroad,* 1880. Pages 75, 79, 80, 81 from *The Innocents Abroad,* 1869. Page 76 from *Extract from Captain Stormfield's Visit to Heaven,* 1909. Pages 83, 114, 122, 123, and 124 from *Following the Equator,* 1896. Page 85 from C. M. Kozlay, *The Lectures of Bret Harte,* 1909. Page 92 courtesy of the National Archives. Page 102 from *The Prince and the Pauper,* 1881. Pages 111, 112, and 113 from *A Connecticut Yankee in King Arthur's Court,* 1889. Page 119 from *Pudd'nhead Wilson,* 1894. Page 130 from Helen Keller, *The Story of My Life,* 1905. Page 133 from *Illustrated London News,* June 1907.

First edition
Published by Chicago Review Press, Incorporated
814 North Franklin Street
Chicago, Illinois 60610
ISBN 1-55652-527-3
Printed in the United States of America
5   4   3   2   1

To Bill Erwin, the youngest kid I know,

and to Zane Shaorui Rasmussen, who is even younger

Contents

Acknowledgments

> "The trouble ain't
> that there is too many fools,
> but that the lightning
> ain't distributed right."
>
> —MARK TWAIN

THE MOST PLEASANT TASK that any author faces is acknowledging the help he has received. I should begin by thanking those who have contributed to my work on Mark Twain, but their number is so great that I cannot name them all. Instead, I'll merely mention the people most directly involved with the present book: Gerilee Hundt, who first suggested it; my agent, Julie Castiglia; and my editor, Cynthia Sherry, whose enthusiastic support has been unflagging. I'm also grateful to Monica Baziuk, who is responsible for the book's beautiful design, and Linda Gray, the book's able copyeditor. Very special thanks also go to Barbara Schmidt and Kevin Bochynski, who read drafts of my manuscript and were ever on hand—as they always are—to answer questions and provide encouragement.

Since this book is for children, I think it appropriate to mention that my interest in Mark Twain goes back to the sad moment my grandfather Alma Rasmussen died and bequeathed to our family a big set of Mark Twain books. From the time I was eight years old until I went to college, I felt privileged to have those books grace a shelf in the bedroom I shared with my brother. Those books advanced my interest in literature and ensured that Mark Twain would always have a special place in my heart. To any parents reading these words, I cannot overstate the importance of book ownership in your children's education. Had my grandfather not left us his books, you would not be holding *Mark Twain for Kids* in your hands right now. Thank you, Grandpa!

Time Line

1835 Samuel Langhorne Clemens, later known as Mark Twain, is born in Florida, Missouri, on November 30

1836 Texas proclaims its independence from Mexico

1837 Victoria becomes queen of Great Britain

1839 Clemens family moves to Hannibal, Missouri

1846–48 United States–Mexican War

1849 California gold rush begins

1853 Sam works as a printer in eastern cities

1857–1861 Sam pilots steamboats on the Mississippi River

1859 Gold is discovered in western Nevada

1860 Abraham Lincoln is elected president

1861–1865 Civil War

1861 Sam goes to Nevada with his brother Orion

1862 Sam becomes a reporter in Virginia City

1863 Sam begins using "Mark Twain" as his pen name

1864 Sam moves to San Francisco

1866 Sam goes to Hawaii

1867 Sam sails to Europe and the Holy Land on the *Quaker City*

The United States buys Alaska from Russia

1868 Ulysses S. Grant is elected president

1869 Sam publishes *The Innocents Abroad*; he becomes part owner of the *Buffalo Express*

First transcontinental railroad is completed

1870 Sam marries Olivia Langdon on February 2

1871 Sam and Olivia move to Hartford, Connecticut

1872 Sam's first daughter is born; he publishes *Roughing It*

1876 *The Adventures of Tom Sawyer* is published

1878–1879 Sam and his family visit Europe

1880 *A Tramp Abroad* is published

1881 *The Prince and the Pauper* is published

1882 Sam revisits the Mississippi River

1883 *Life on the Mississippi* is published

1884 *Adventures of Huckleberry Finn* is published

1889 *A Connecticut Yankee in King Arthur's Court* is published

1891–1900 Sam lives abroad with his family

1894 *Pudd'nhead Wilson* and *Tom Sawyer Abroad* are published

1895–1896 Sam undertakes an around-the-world lecture tour

1896 Sam's daughter Susy dies; *Tom Sawyer, Detective* and *Personal Reflections of Joan of Arc* are published

1897 *Following the Equator* is published

1898 Spanish-American War

United States annexes Hawaii

1899–1902 South African War

1900 Sam returns to the United States with his family

1901 Queen Victoria dies

1904 Olivia dies

1907 Sam receives an honorary Oxford University degree

1908 Sam settles in Redding, Connecticut

1910 Sam dies at his Redding home on April 21

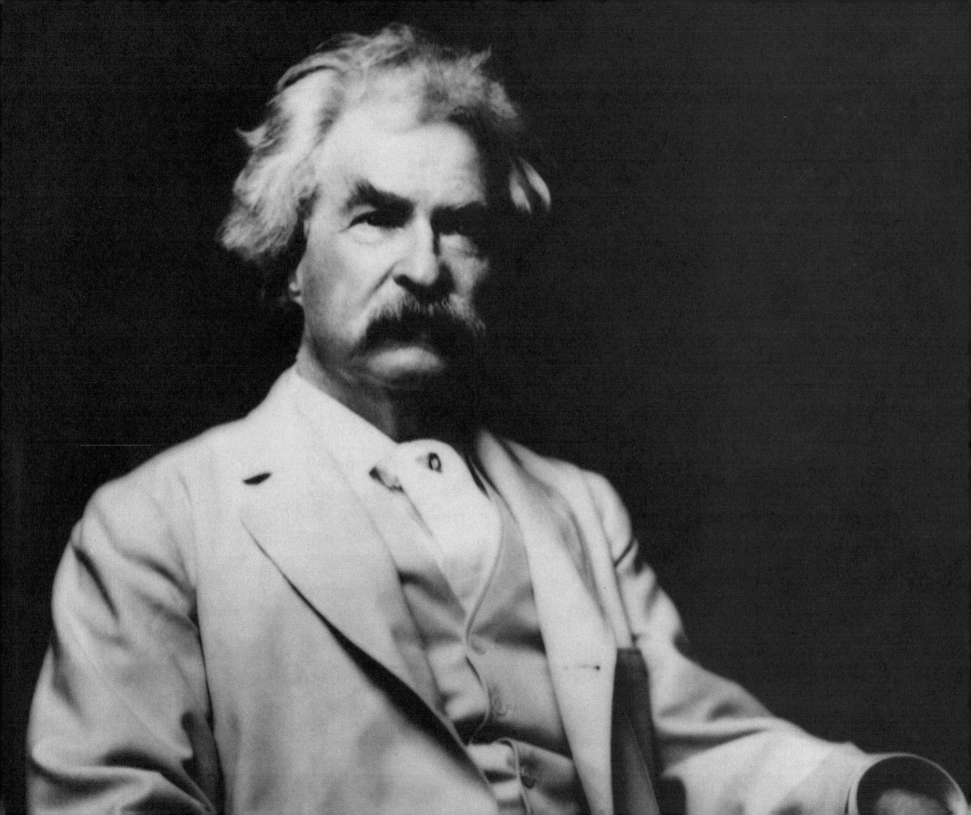

Introduction

What Makes Mark Twain Important

IT HAS BEEN NEARLY 100 YEARS since Samuel Langhorne Clemens—the man best remembered as Mark Twain—died. During his last years, he ranked as one of the most famous and beloved people of his time. Through four decades, people around the world had read and laughed at his books and stories and roared with delight at his public speeches. By the turn of the 20th century, his face was more widely recognized than those of most U.S. presidents.

In that bygone age, long before the rise of movies, radio, television, and music recordings, Mark Twain was much like a modern-day "superstar." Wherever he went, he was followed by reporters and fans, and almost everything that he said in public was quoted around the world. The great inventor Thomas Alva Edison once summed up the nation's feelings about Mark Twain when he said, "The average American loves his family. If he has any love left over for some other person, he generally selects Mark Twain."

When we look back on Mark Twain's life, it may not seem surprising that he remains famous and beloved even today. The names of his most famous characters, Tom Sawyer and Huckleberry Finn, are as familiar to us as those of George Washington and Abraham Lincoln. It is a rare American who has never read a book by Mark Twain, and someone rarer still who has never seen a movie that is based on one of his books.

Mark Twain's books made people laugh during his lifetime, and a big part of the reason

that his books continue to be read is that they still make us laugh, all these years later. However, there is much more to Mark Twain and his books than their humor. In addition to making us laugh, his most enduring works have helped us to understand what it means to be American. Although Mark Twain was one of the most popular authors of his day, most people at that time regarded him only as a funnyman. They would be surprised to know that a century later his books are not only still popular, but considered serious and important as well.

Many people now argue that Mark Twain's *Adventures of Huckleberry Finn* is the greatest American novel ever written—a view that novelist Ernest Hemingway was one of the first to express in 1935. In *Green Hills of Africa*, Hemingway wrote:

> → *All modern American literature comes from one book by Mark Twain called* Huckleberry Finn. . . . *it's the best book we've had. All American writing comes from that. There was nothing before. There has been nothing as good since.* ←

People have argued over what Hemingway meant when he wrote those words, but the most likely explanation is that he was thinking of the naturalness of Mark Twain's writing.

Adventures of Huckleberry Finn is narrated in the voice of Huck, an ignorant backwoods Missouri boy. *Adventures of Huckleberry Finn* is a powerful story, and its power is made stronger by the naturalness of Huck's narration. Huck isn't trying to sound like a literary writer. When we read the book, Huck seems like a close friend who is talking to us. He is simply speaking as he normally does, and saying exactly what he is thinking. Many later writers, including Hemingway, followed Mark Twain's example of writing in a natural voice in their own books.

Toward the end of his life, Mark Twain pointed out that, of the 220,000 books published in the United States over the previous century, those that were "still alive and marketable" wouldn't even fill a bathtub. There is some truth to that observation. Most books—including most bestsellers—are quickly forgotten, regardless of how popular they are when they first come out. Why, then, are most of Mark Twain's books still read and enjoyed? Yes, some are "assigned reading" in schools, but that is only part of the reason. The more important reason we continue to read Mark Twain's books is that his words still have the power to touch us—to make us laugh, make us cry, or move us in other ways.

The Adventures of Tom Sawyer is one of the great adventure stories of all time, and it is a book that both adults and children enjoy. *Adventures of Huckleberry Finn* is an equally great adventure, and it, too, is filled with wonderful humor and warm human compassion. It is the kind of book that changes the ways that people regard other human beings. *The Prince and the Pauper*, another great adventure story, offers not one, but three heroes. It's a fantasy story, featuring some real historical figures and set in 16th-century England, that is fun to read because it lets us imagine what it may have been like to be a king.

As great as his books are, there is much more to Mark Twain than his writing. He was what some might call a "Renaissance man"—the type of person who is interested in almost everybody and everything. He had a long and exciting life that took him from what he called the backwoods of Missouri to the Mississippi River, the gold and silver fields of the West, the great cities of the East, and other places around the world. He spent about 12 years of his life outside the United States, and he crossed the Atlantic Ocean 25 times, during an age when few Americans even left their county. He knew many of the great literary, business, and political leaders of his time, and he dined with presidents, kings, and emperors. He was fascinated by history, science, and technology, and he not only wrote about these subjects, but kept up with the latest developments in his everyday life. He flew in a hot-air balloon, was one of the first writers to use a typewriter, had one of the first private telephones in the world, and patented several inventions of his own.

To read about Mark Twain is to read about the history of the whole world during his time. There is almost no end to the fascinating things connected to this remarkable man.

Note to the Reader

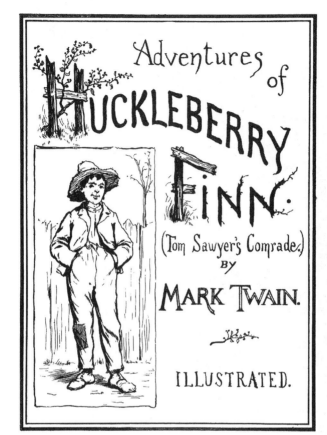

"MARK TWAIN" was not the real name of the author of *The Adventures of Tom Sawyer* and *Adventures of Huckleberry Finn*. He was named Samuel Langhorne Clemens when he was born and went by that name until the day he died. He started using "Mark Twain" as his pen name—the name he put on things that he wrote—when he was 27 years old. However, he never tried to hide the fact that his real name was Clemens, and he was known to the public by both names. In fact, his real name appeared in most of his books, sometimes directly below his pen name on the title page. It can be confusing to know what to call him. Perhaps it will help to remember that, while he was "Mark Twain" during only part of his life, he was *always* "Sam Clemens"—and that is what we shall call him most of the time in this book.

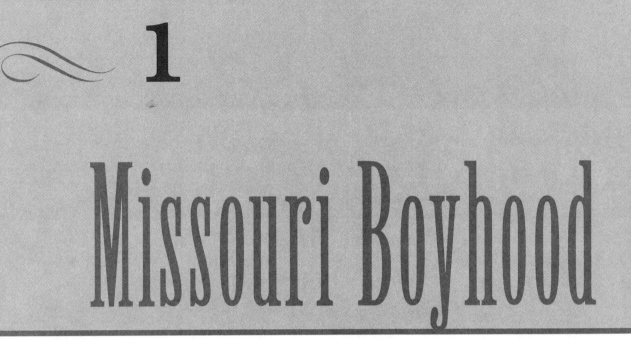

1
Missouri Boyhood

Samuel Langhorne Clemens first saw the light of day in the north-eastern Missouri village of Florida—a place so small that he later called it "nearly invisible." It had a population of only 100 people when he was born. When he grew up, he bragged that not only had he single-handedly raised the village's population by one percent, but he could have done the same for *any* town. Wild exaggerations like that would someday become a trademark of Mark Twain's humor.

Like most people of his time, Sam was born in his family's home—a two-room house that was little larger than a shack. The date was November 30, 1835. At that time, Andrew Jackson was president of the United States, the nation's frontier began just west of the Mississippi River, and government troops were busy fighting the Seminole Indians of Florida.

Sam's father named him after his own father, Samuel B. Clemens, who died long before Sam was born. When Sam's grandfather was only 35 years old, he was crushed by a rolling log while helping neighbors build a log cabin in a Virginia county that later became part of West Virginia.

Family history would later find fictional expression in many of the books that Sam was to write. Indeed, the history of his family's move from Tennessee to Missouri is the starting point of *The Gilded Age*, a novel that he wrote with his friend Charles Dudley Warner in 1873. In that novel, the members of the fictional Hawkins family are modeled on the Clemenses, and Sam's own fictional counterpart is Clay Hawkins.

Sam's father came from a family that was proud of its elite ancestry. Sam himself liked to boast about one ancestor, an Englishman named Geoffrey Clement, who helped to have England's King Charles I beheaded in the 17th century. Sam's mother's side of the family also claimed noble descent; they were related to an English family named Lambton (which became "Lampton" when the family emigrated to America), whose men were heirs to an earldom. Sam's interest in noble descent shows up in several of his novels. The most famous examples can be found in *Adventures of Huckleberry Finn*. One of that novel's two

Mark Twain's Birthplace

AMAZINGLY, THE TINY wood-frame house in which Sam was born in Florida, Missouri, still exists. It is now protected inside a modern museum. Interestingly, the museum is only a stone's throw from the beautiful Mark Twain Lake, which was created after the Salt River was dammed in 1966. It had been John Clemens's dream to develop the river, but he could never have imagined that one day, such a development would include a great body of water named after his own son.

☞ **Mark Twain's birthplace as it looked around 1900.**

scoundrels claims to be the rightful duke of Bridgewater, and the other, the king of France. Much of the fun of the story comes from Huck's pretending to believe the scoundrels' outrageous claims.

Sam's father, John Marshall Clemens, was born in Virginia in 1798. He was named after the prominent Virginian John Marshall, who later became a famous chief justice of the United States. However, John Clemens had a hard childhood. After the early death of his father, his mother remarried and moved to Kentucky, and he was soon forced to go to work. Eventually, he had to give most of what he had inherited from his father to his stepfather in return for raising him. With what he had left, he married Jane Lampton, of Kentucky, in 1823. Two years later, they moved across the border into Tennessee, where all five of Sam's older siblings were born.

The Clemenses lived in several different Tennessee towns. John Clemens held some important government jobs and had a small law practice. He even saved enough money to buy more than 100 square miles of land in eastern Tennessee, as an investment for his family's future.

During the early 1830s, Jane Clemens's sister Patsy and her husband, John Quarles, moved from Tennessee to the town of Florida, in northeastern Missouri. There they estab-lished a small farm and ran a general store. The Quarleses thought that Florida's future was bright, and they encouraged the Clemenses to follow them there. Around the middle of 1835, John and Jane Clemens left Tennessee and joined their relatives in Missouri. Sam was born in Florida, Missouri, about six months after they arrived. His only younger brother, Henry, was also born there, three years later.

During their first few years in Missouri, things went well for the Clemenses. Sam's father helped his brother-in-law run his store, then established his own dry-goods store. He also became a community leader. He had important jobs on a committee that was orga-nized to develop navigation on the nearby Salt River, which fed into the Mississippi, and on another committee that was working to bring the railroad to Florida. He also became a coun-try judge. If Florida became the prosperous center of commerce that they envisioned, the family's future would be bright.

However, the town did not prosper, and the Clemenses suffered for it. The Salt River never became important, and no railroad line ever reached the town. In fact, Florida never grew much larger than it was then. John Clemens's efforts to develop a law practice and run a store failed. To make matters worse, Sam's nine-year-old sister, Margaret, died in 1839. A few months later, John Clemens sold his prop-

The two most famous scoundrels in *Adventures of Huckleberry Finn*; one (left) claims to be the king of France, the other the duke of Bridgewater.

Mark Twain's Descendants

A PERSON'S DIRECT DESCENDANTS are his or her children, grandchildren, great-grandchildren, and so on. They do not include nephews and nieces and their descendants. Although no direct descendants of Mark Twain are still living, we occasionally hear about a person (such as a certain New York Yankee baseball player) who claims to be one. The fact that all such claims are false can be easily shown by looking at the Clemens family tree: Only the five people whose names appear in **color** below Samuel L. Clemens's name are his *direct* descendants. These consist of his four children and his only granddaughter, Nina. Since Nina died in 1966 without leaving any children of her own, she was Sam's last direct descendant. Annie Moffett and Samuel Moffett—Mark Twain's niece and nephew—do have living descendants. Those people are related to Mark Twain, but they are not his direct descendants.

Family trees, which show connections among relatives, are like real trees, with branches growing out in all directions. This family tree shows five generations of Mark Twain's relatives, from his grandparents to his only grandchild.

Samuel B. Clemens 1770–1805	**Pamela Goggin** 1775–1844	**Benjamin Lampton** 1770–1837	**Margaret Casey** 1783–1818

John M. Clemens 1798–1847 ◄······► **Jane Lampton** 1803–1890

| **Orion Clemens** 1825–1897 | **Mollie Stotts** 1834–1904 | **Pamela Clemens** 1827–1904 | **William Moffett** 1816–1865 | **Pleasant Clemens** 1828/29 | **Margaret Clemens** 1830–1839 | **Benjamin Clemens** 1832–1842 | **Samuel L. Clemens** 1835–1910 | **Olivia Langdon** 1845–1904 | **Henry Clemens** 1838–1858 |

| **Jennie Clemens** 1855–1864 | **Annie Moffett** 1852–1950 | **Samuel Moffett** 1860–1908 | **Langdon Clemens** 1870–1872 | **Susy Clemens** 1872–1896 | **Clara Clemens** 1874–1962 | **Ossip Gabrilowitsch** 1878–1936 | **Jean Clemens** 1880–1909 |

Nina Gabrilowitsch 1910–1966

Jane

Pamela

Orion

Henry

erty and moved the family to Hannibal, Missouri, a larger town on the Mississippi River, about 35 miles northeast of Florida.

The Family Moves to Hannibal

S AM WAS NOT QUITE four years old when the family moved to Hannibal. He couldn't have remembered Florida well from the time his family lived there. However, almost every year he lived in Hannibal, his family returned to Florida during the summer to stay on the Quarleses' farm. Florida thus remained important to Sam throughout his childhood. The fic-

tional Mississippi riverfront village of St. Petersburg that is featured in Sam's best-known books, *The Adventures of Tom Sawyer* and *Adventures of Huckleberry Finn*, is modeled after the town of Hannibal. However, St. Petersburg also contains many elements of Florida, and of the Quarles farm.

Most of what we know about Sam's childhood comes from his own writings, especially the long, rambling autobiography that he wrote and dictated toward the end of his life. The stories of his youth that he told are rich and colorful, but they aren't always reliable. Sam always liked to take a good story and make it better, whether the result was true or not. His talent for doing this is one of the things that makes his books fun to read.

☛ Tom Sawyer's house (left) was designed to resemble the real house in which Sam grew up in Hannibal.

However, that same talent also makes it difficult for us to know what to believe about his recollections about his early life.

One of the reasons that *The Adventures of Tom Sawyer* has become a beloved classic is that it offers a joyous picture of a time and place that seems like a paradise for the children, particularly the boys, who are at the center of all the novel's adventures. Tom and his friends enjoy fishing, swimming, rafting, watching circuses and traveling troupes of actors, and playing adventure games such as pretending to be Robin Hood. Tom never has to look very far to find a companion with whom to share an adventure, and every time the novel places a dangerous challenge in his path, he emerges triumphant. *The Adventures of Tom Sawyer* is one of the most satisfying boyhood adventure stories ever written, and the book has made Sam's boyhood home of Hannibal famous as a symbol of American values during a simpler time. However, the real Hannibal of Sam Clemens's boyhood in Missouri wasn't quite the paradise that the fictional St. Petersburg is. In fact, a careful read of *The Adventures of Tom Sawyer* reveals that St. Petersburg itself can be a dangerous and scary place.

In the real world of Sam Clemens's youth during the mid-19th century, life was far harder than it is now. This was especially true along the frontier, of which Missouri was still a part during the 1830s and 1840s. People had to work hard merely to get by. There was no electricity. Water didn't come from taps; it had to be pumped by hand. Stoves and heaters burned wood, which had to be chopped, carried, lighted, and tended. Most of the food that people ate didn't come from grocery stores, but from gardens and farms, and it required hard work to produce. If a harsh winter or other disaster damaged crops, times could be tough, indeed.

People who didn't produce their own food and clothes needed money or goods to trade for the items they required. For John Clemens to prosper as a merchant, there had to be customers to buy his goods. When times were tough, everyone in the community felt the pinch.

In addition to facing an uncertain economic future, the real Hannibal was a place in which violence—even murder—was common. It was also a place in which diseases such as measles, cholera, and typhoid periodically threatened to wipe out large parts of the population. Although *The Adventures of Tom Sawyer* suggests a picture of carefree life for boys, it also hints at the danger that existed in a town like Hannibal.

Tom Sawyer's war games.

ever, they also gave him ideas that he would later use in his books.

While *The Adventures of Tom Sawyer* is generally a cheerful story in which mostly good things happen to its young hero, it has an undercurrent of danger. Early in the story, Tom and Huck go to a graveyard at night to try out a magical cure for warts. There they happen to see a doctor and two other men dig up a recently buried body. The grave robbers get into an argument, and one of them (Injun Joe) kills the doctor while the third man, Muff Potter, is passed out.

What Tom and Huck see that night nearly scares them to death. The next day they return to the graveyard, where the villagers are gathering to look at the murder scene. When Injun Joe says that Muff killed the doctor, Tom and Huck are amazed that God doesn't strike Joe dead for lying, and they become even more afraid of him than ever. They run off together and sign an oath in their own blood, swearing never to tell their terrible secret to anyone else. Huck is afraid that if he or Tom tells their secret, and Injun Joe isn't hanged, "Why, he'd kill us some time or other, just as dead sure as we're a-laying here."

Even though Tom and Huck renew their pledge to keep their secret, Tom becomes a witness at Muff's murder trial and must reveal the truth. The moment he tells everyone that Injun

Judging by the many violent events that Sam witnessed when he was growing up, Hannibal was anything but a completely safe place. With his own eyes, he saw several murders, several attempted murders, a hanging, an attempted lynching, and a man burned to death in a jail. He also saw friends drown, and he came close to drowning himself several times. Those awful experiences gave him nightmares that haunted him for years. How-

Joe killed the doctor, Joe jumps out the court-room window and disappears. Afterward, Tom is treated as a hero for saving Muff, but he is now haunted by even scarier nightmares. When Tom finally meets Joe again, in a dark cave, the effect is electric. If Sam Clemens's own boyhood had been less scary, it's doubtful that he would have written scenes such as these.

Several scenes in *Adventures of Huckleberry Finn* describe other violent incidents that Sam saw as a boy. In one, a man named Boggs is shot simply for pestering a man. Sam's description of Boggs's death is an almost exact duplicate of his recollections of the murder of a real Hannibal man named Smarr. Boggs, like Smarr, is shot in the chest and laid down on a floor, and someone places a heavy Bible on his chest, thinking that God's words will comfort him. Sam grew up having nightmares about Smarr's murder.

While *The Adventures of Tom Sawyer* at least acknowledges the existence of violence and danger in the fictional St. Petersburg, it barely hints at another unhappy reality of Sam Clemens's boyhood village: African American slavery. Like all the states of the pre–Civil War South, Missouri permitted people to own other human beings as their property, just as one might own a horse or a piece of furniture. The first hint in *The Adventures of Tom Sawyer* that slavery exists in St. Petersburg is

☛ Injun Joe bursts through the courtroom window.

☛ When Sam was about 10, he sneaked into his father's dark justice-of-the-peace office one night and gradually realized that a dead man was lying on the floor. The man had been stabbed to death, and his body was placed in John Clemens's office until an inquest could be held.

the brief appearance of a "small colored boy" named Jim, who does chores for Aunt Polly. A second hint is a footnote in a later chapter, which explains the difference between how dogs and slaves were named in Sam's time.

Harry Potter and Tom Sawyer

THE MOST FAMOUS CHARACTER in modern children's literature is undoubtedly author J. K. Rowling's boy wizard, Harry Potter. Harry's name has become a household word—much like that of one of his most important literary ancestors, Tom Sawyer. People who have read both *The Adventures of Tom Sawyer* and the Harry Potter novels cannot help noticing striking similarities between the two boys:

☞ Both boys are around eleven years old when their adventures begin.

☞ Both boys are orphans being raised by their mothers' sisters.

☞ Harry lives with a spoiled cousin, Dudley, whom he cannot stand; Tom lives with a goody-goody half-brother, Sid, whom he cannot stand.

☞ Until Harry learns that he is a wizard, he leads an ordinary ("muggle") life and knows nothing about magic; Tom also leads an ordinary life, but he is always ready to try out magic spells.

☞ The friends with whom Harry shares his most thrilling adventures are a boy, Ron, and a girl, Hermione; Tom shares his adventures with Huck Finn and Becky Thatcher.

☞ While both boys are essentially respectful, they're not above breaking rules during emergencies.

☞ Like the first five Harry Potter stories, which reach their climaxes in dark dungeons and similar settings, *The Adventures of Tom Sawyer* reaches its dramatic climax deep inside a pitch-dark cave, where Tom confronts the evil Injun Joe.

African Americans in Sam's Life

S AM GREW UP AROUND SLAVES. His own family owned several when he was a boy. In fact, he modeled "Jim," a character in *The Adventures of Tom Sawyer*, on a family slave named Sandy. In his autobiography, he later recalled how Sandy's nonstop singing once drove him nearly crazy with distraction. When he complained to his mother about it, she had the sensitivity to appreciate Sandy's unhappiness. She explained to Sam that when Sandy sang, it meant he wasn't remembering his mother, whom he would never see again.

Sam was descended from slaveowners on both sides of his family. When his parents married in 1823, each of them already owned a few slaves. Over the years, they bought and sold other slaves, and they didn't always treat them well. In fact, Sam's father was capable of ruthlessly beating his slaves—a fact that Sam later chose to forget.

→ *In my schoolboy days I had no aversion to slavery. I was not aware that there was anything wrong about it. No one arraigned it in my hearing; the local papers said nothing against it; the local pulpit taught us that God approved it, that it was a holy thing, and that the doubter need only look in the Bible if he wished to settle his mind—and then the texts were read aloud to us to make the matter sure; if the slaves themselves had an aversion to slavery, they were wise and said nothing. In Hannibal we seldom saw a slave misused; on the farm, never.* ←

The last sentence reveals how Sam could look at the past through rose-tinted glasses. Slaves *were* misused in Hannibal. In fact, his own father was not only an occasionally cruel master, he was also a strong enemy of abolitionists—people who worked to free slaves and to abolish slavery itself. It says a great deal about the kind of man that Sam became that he would grow up not only to despise slavery, but also to believe that it was the duty of every white person to make up for the terrible wrongs that had been done to African Americans.

Sam's warm feelings about black people came from his close associations with slaves during his youth, especially during the summers that he spent on his uncle's farm. He and the other white children played games with the black children on nearly equal terms. Sam especially liked an old slave known as Uncle Daniel, "whose sympathies were wide and warm, and whose heart was honest and simple and knew no guile." At night, all the

children liked to gather around the fire in Daniel's kitchen and listen to him tell wonderful stories. Sam would later use Daniel's stories in own writings, and when he created the heroic character Jim for *Adventures of Huckleberry Finn*, he was thinking mostly of Uncle Daniel.

It was thus mainly on the farm that Sam developed his strong liking for black people and his appreciation of their fine qualities.

Slavery in Missouri

MISSOURI GAINED STATEHOOD in August 1821 under terms of the Missouri Compromise, which permitted it to become a slave-holding state, while Maine was admitted to the Union at the same time as a free state. Although slavery was legal in Missouri, many people there, particularly those in the northern counties, opposed it. Indeed, it was Missouri's mixed feelings about slavery that began the Dred Scott case, which led to the controversial U.S. Supreme Court ruling in 1857 that the Missouri Compromise was unconstitutional. Dred Scott was a Missouri slave who, many years earlier, had gone with his master to live in a free state and in a free territory and then returned to Missouri. After his master died in 1848, Scott went to court to sue for his freedom, arguing that, since he had lived in places where slavery was outlawed, he was a free man in Missouri. His case went all the way to the Supreme Court, where he lost. The Court's decision ruled that black slaves were mere property and could never have the same rights as American citizens. Missouri's split over slavery came to the surface with the outbreak of the Civil War.

> "If your mother tells you to do a thing, it is wrong to reply that you won't. It is better and more becoming to intimate that you will do as she bids you, and then afterwards act quietly in the matter according to the dictates of your better judgment."
>
> —MARK TWAIN

Sixty years later, he wrote that the "black face is as welcome to me now as it was then." As an adult, Sam would favor full civil rights for African Americans, and he quietly funded an African American law student's education at Yale.

Health Hazards

IN ADDITION to the violence and social injustice that Sam saw as he was growing up, he lived during an era in which people were terrified by the constant threat of disease. He would live to see revolutionary changes in the medical sciences. But when he was still a boy, European and American medicine hadn't advanced much beyond the few discoveries that had been made by the ancient Greeks.

In the mid-19th century, little was known about how diseases spread, and still less was known about how to prevent or cure them. Inoculations against disease were only beginning to be understood. There were no antibiotics, and there were few drugs that really helped to prevent or cure anything. Consequently, people living along the western frontier had little confidence that their children would survive. Families usually had large numbers of children to ensure that at least some would reach adulthood.

Sam himself was the sixth of his parents' seven children. He had four brothers and two sisters. One brother, Pleasant, died in infancy about six years before Sam was born, and his name was almost forgotten in the family. Another brother and a sister also died while Sam was still young. Only his oldest brother, Orion, his oldest sister, Pamela, and his younger brother, Henry, made it to adulthood. Sam would not only outlive all of them, he would also outlive three of his own four children, as well as his wife.

Sam developed a strong interest in medicine and a deep concern for the loss of loved ones. This is reflected in the characters in his novels and stories. Tom Sawyer is an orphan whose only sibling is a half-brother, Sid. Huck Finn is an only child whose only living parent is an abusive father who is rarely around. Many of Sam's other stories also feature orphaned characters.

The early deaths of three of Sam's six siblings were typical of family losses of that time. According to Clemens family lore, the biggest surprise was that Sam himself survived childhood. Born about two months premature, he seemed too weak to last long, and there were health scares aplenty in the Missouri of his youth. In fact, his parents apparently considered settling in St. Louis when they first came to Missouri in 1835, but they continued on to the village of Florida, perhaps because of a cholera scare in the state's biggest city. Cholera is a dangerous bacterial disease that spreads rapidly in crowded places—which is why a place like St. Louis could be dangerous to live in. Cholera returned to the Mississippi Valley during the 1840s, scaring people so badly that Sam later said that for each person killed by cholera, three more died of fright.

When Sam was about 10, a measles epidemic swept through his town and carried off a child almost every day. As he later recalled, "The mothers of the town were nearly demented with fright." His own mother—who had already lost three children—did everything she could to protect her three youngest children from coming into contact with the disease.

Sam's mother did such a good job of scaring him that he found the suspense of waiting to see if measles would claim him unbearable. He later said that he made up his mind to end the suspense and settle the matter, one way or the other, and be done with it. His closest friend, Will Bowen, had a bad case of measles, and Sam sneaked into Will's house and climbed into bed with him. When Will's mother discovered him there, she quickly sent him home. He came back a second time, however, and managed to get a case of measles that nearly killed him.

Market Your Own Patent Medicine

During the 19th century, concoctions that supposedly cured almost every ailment were popular throughout the United States. Called patent medicines, they had names such as "Perry Davis's Pain-Killer," "Dr. Pierce's Golden Medical Discovery," "Doan's Kidney Pills," "Hamlin's Wizard Oil," and "Dr. Parmenter's Magnetic Oil." Most of these patent medicines contained only useless (and, luckily, harmless) ingredients, but many people who took them believed that they worked. The reason was simple: The human body recovers from most common illnesses whether it receives medical treatment or not. People who took patent medicines thought that the *medicine* had cured them, however, and they were happy to write glowing endorsements. Salesmen used these endorsements to sell more of their useless "medicine."

WHAT YOU NEED
* Mixing bowl
* Sugar
* Water
* Food coloring
* Empty, clean bottles with lids
* Felt-tip pen
* Plain adhesive labels that you can write on
* Writing paper

In a mixing bowl, make enough sugar water to fill your bottles. Dissolve approximately one tablespoon of granulated sugar in each cup of water used. Stir in a few drops of food coloring. Use whatever color you like. Fill the bottles with sugar water and cap them.

Think of an appealing name for your patent medicine, and print it carefully on adhesive labels. Attach a label to each bottle. Next, write an advertisement for your medicine. Your ad should list all the ailments that the medicine can "cure" (such as colds, rheumatism, dandruff, or backaches). It should also include endorsements, which you can write as if they had come from satisfied users, that rave about the good things that the medicine has done for them.

Dangerous Waters

PASSING EPIDEMICS weren't the only things that made Sam's early life dangerous. Accidents were always possible, and the Clemenses lived not far from one of the greatest sources of accidents imaginable: the Mississippi River. During the summers, Sam and his friends loved to fish, swim, and boat in the river and its local feeder, Bear Creek. During the winter they enjoyed skating and playing on the ice.

More than one of Sam's playmates drowned in the creek or the river, and others experienced serious mishaps there. One winter night, Sam and his friend Tom Nash were skating far out on the frozen Mississippi when they heard the ice start to break up. Sam made it back to the shore, but Tom fell into the frigid water. He survived, but got sick with scarlet fever, which made him lose his hearing.

Sam later made frequent use of drowning incidents in his writings, and he often created characters who are deaf, or who pretend to be deaf. Most of his deaf characters are victims of scarlet fever, such as 'Lizabeth, the "deef" daughter of the slave Jim in *Adventures of Huckleberry Finn*.

Apt to run off with his friends and take foolish chances, as he did on the ice, Sam caused his mother considerable anxiety. She feared for her children's health and was fascinated with "patent" medicines. Her concerns are reflected in Tom Sawyer's Aunt Polly. When Tom is not feeling well, Polly doses him with "Pain-Killer," a new patent medicine. Tom describes it as "simply fire in a liquid form." One of the novel's funniest moments occurs when Tom gives his dose of medicine to the family cat—exactly as Sam himself once did when he was a boy.

When Sam was well along in years himself, his mother (who lived to be 80) once said to

☞ **The results of Tom's dosing his cat with "Pain-Killer."**

him, "You gave me more uneasiness than any child I had." He replied, "I suppose you were afraid I wouldn't live," and she surprised him by saying, "No; afraid you would!"

Games That Sam Played

THE CLEMENS FAMILY was poor, but they were not much worse off than their neighbors. Sam didn't grow up thinking of himself as poor. By and large, his childhood appears to have been happy. Surrounded by friends and living in a natural playground, without having to work hard at anything, he had ample opportunities for fun, much like the boys in *The Adventures of Tom Sawyer*. That novel describes all kinds of sports that Sam had enjoyed as a boy, including swimming, fishing, kite-flying, and shooting marbles, as well as games he played such as pretending to be armies, law courts, steamboat pilots, Robin Hood, and others.

Sam always had a special interest in pirates. When he was a boy, he fantasized about growing up to become a pirate, and he loved to play pirate games on the river. One of the most fun episodes of *The Adventures of Tom Sawyer* is

☛ Tom Sawyer's pirate band.

the part in which Tom, Huck, and Joe Harper sneak away from their village, borrow a raft, and float down to Jackson's Island, where they spend several days pretending to be pirates. They have a wonderful time, but, like real little boys, they soon become homesick. When Sam was older, he claimed to be descended from pirates, and he added that he wasn't ashamed of it. This was another example of the kinds of exaggerations he enjoyed. He didn't really expect people to believe him.

Playing hooky.

School Days

OF THE MANY remarkable things about Sam, one of the most impressive is that he was largely self-taught. Not only did he never go to college, he also never went to high school. The only real schooling he received when he was young was limited. Public schools were rare in small towns when he was a boy. Instead, villages like Hannibal typically had tiny, privately run schools. Sam attended two such schools in Hannibal. He also occasionally attended another small school during the summers his family spent in Florida, Missouri.

As you might imagine, the education that children got in such schools wasn't rigorous. The schools usually had only one teacher, who tried to instruct children of all ages—and occasionally adults, too—in a single room. Books and other school supplies were limited, and students often wouldn't show up for class at all. Pupils received little individual atten-

> "In the first place God made idiots. This was for practice. Then He made School Boards."
>
> —MARK TWAIN

tion, and little was expected of them. Teachers emphasized memorizing facts, mastering spelling and penmanship, and learning the most basic math calculations. Students did much of their writing with chalk on their own slates, which were like tiny blackboards that could be wiped clean and reused.

Like many children, Sam hated going to school. He made a fine art out of playing hooky. Sometimes his mother tried to make it more difficult for him to cut school to go swimming by sewing his shirt collars together in the morning and checking to see if the threads were broken in the evening. (In *The Adventures of Tom Sawyer*, Tom tries to fool Aunt Polly by resewing his collar himself, but he gets punished after Sid points out to Polly that the color of the thread has changed.) As much as he disliked school, however, Sam must have been a good pupil. He later recalled that he won his school's spelling medal almost every week, while his friend John Robards was the regular winner of the medal for "amiability." Each week's winners got to wear their medals through the following week. This suited Sam's thirst for glory.

Sam seems to have struggled with math, though, and he especially disliked the multiplication table. He later shared his dislike of multiplication with Huck Finn. After Huck goes to school for several months, he explains that he can "say the multiplication table up to 'six times seven is thirty-five,'" but he doesn't reckon he "could ever get any further than that if I was to live forever."

Love of Reading

THE MOST IMPORTANT THING that Sam learned in school was a love of reading. He didn't have access to a wide variety of books, but he seems to have read everything he could find. At his Sunday school, children could earn tickets by reciting memorized Bible verses, then exchange the tickets for the privilege of borrowing books from their teacher's collection. Although Sam hated Sunday school at least as much as he hated regular school, he was eager to get at the books, so he regularly reeled off five verses for his kindly old teacher, who never seemed to notice that Sam recited the *same* five verses every Sunday.

The books that Sam borrowed from the Sunday-school teacher were about goody-goody characters whom he found boring. However, he later recalled that even these characters were "better society than none, and I was glad to have their company and disapprove of it." When he was 40, he created the kind of book he would have preferred to read when he was young: *The Adventures of Tom Sawyer*. This was one of the first American novels about a boy who wasn't a goody-goody. Tom not only ignores authority and repeatedly gets into trouble, he even triumphs over better-behaved children. In one famous scene, Tom persuades his Sunday-school classmates to give him the tickets that they have struggled to earn by memorizing Bible verses. He uses their hard-earned tickets to claim a coveted prize and win a few minutes of public glory. It is the sort of trick that Sam might have played on his friends when he was a boy.

The love of reading that Sam developed as a child stayed with him until the day he died. He preferred adventure stories, such as Ned Buntline's popular "dime novels" about pirates and cowboys and Indians. However, he was satisfied reading whatever books he could find. As he grew up, he came to prefer biographies and histories and did not read a great deal of fiction. Reading opened his eyes to the world, taught him about language, and fostered his love of learning. He probably got his love of learning from his mother. After she died in 1890, he wrote that "to the very day of her death she felt a strong interest in the whole world and everything and everybody in it."

☞ Sam was a constant reader throughout his life.

Make a Slate

Nowadays, we think nothing of writing a few lines on a sheet of paper, then crumpling it up, discarding it, and continuing our work on a fresh sheet. However, paper was a precious commodity in young Sam Clemens's time, particularly in rural regions. When he was a boy in school, Sam saw little paper and did most of his writing on slates, miniature chalkboards that students could use over and over. Students did most of their assignments on their slates, which they wiped clean after their teachers inspected their work. This is where the expression "starting with a clean slate" comes from.

Slates take their name from the type of rock from which most of them were made. A fine-grained mineral, slate can be split into thin, flat sheets that make ideal surfaces for writing. Writing slates generally had wood frames to protect their brittle edges and to make them easier to hold. Students wrote on them with chalk or special slate pencils, which were similar to today's crayons and grease pencils. You can make your own real slate if you have access to a building-supply store that sells slate tiles for roofing. It's easy to make an imitation slate using more readily available materials, however.

WHAT YOU NEED

* 1 or 2 9-by-12-inch pieces of heavy cardboard
* Glue, if necessary
* Scissors
* Solid-colored (preferably white), slick-surfaced, self-adhesive shelf paper
* Paper punch
* Piece of strong string, about 20 inches long
* Grease pencil or water-based felt-tip pen
* Rag

Test the cardboard's strength. If one piece of the cardboard isn't strong enough to withstand bending when you hold it in one hand and write on its surface with the other hand, glue two pieces of cardboard together.

Cut a piece of the shelf paper into a 12-by-15-inch rectangle. Lay it flat on a table, with the adhesive side up, and carefully peel off the protective backing so that the adhesive is exposed. Center the cardboard on the paper and press it flat, so that its back sticks to the paper.

Use scissors to cut notches in each corner of the paper, as shown in the diagram. Gently pull the flaps of the paper over the edges of the cardboard, then turn the cardboard over and press firmly on the paper, working any bubbles in the paper toward the edges. Be careful not to let the flaps stick on anything. Turn the cardboard over again. Pull the paper flaps tightly over the cardboard and press them into place.

Punch a hole in the upper right corner of the board if you are right-handed, or in the upper left corner if you are left-handed. Tie one end of the string to the hole in the board. Tie the other end to the end of the felt-tip pen or grease pencil. Use the rag as an eraser.

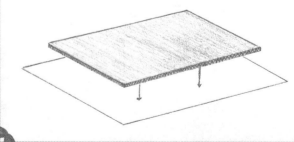

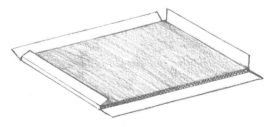

The same may be said of Sam himself, for one of his chief characteristics was the breadth of his interest in the world. He would eventually write about almost everything you can imagine: people, history, science, literature, technology, language, and much more. He became a keen observer, and he developed a wonderful ability to describe things in vivid detail.

After his father died in 1847, Sam stayed in school for about two years, then quit before he turned 14—about the same age as a modern-day ninth-grader. However, while his formal schooling may have ended then, that moment was the beginning of his real education. Throughout the rest of his life, he continued to learn, through the jobs that he held, the people that he met, and the many places to which he traveled, and by continuing to read as much as he could.

The Apprentice Printer

OF THE MANY CAREERS that Sam would have, the first was that of a printer. He began that career when he was about 12, working for the tiny newspapers of Hannibal, including one owned for a few years by his brother Orion. In fact, Sam also began his writing career in those same newspaper printing shops while he was still a teenager. At that time, there were no such things as radio, television, or telephones, and newspapers were the most important means of communicating news. Virtually every city and town in America had at least one newspaper, and even towns as small as Hannibal often had several.

One of Sam's main printing jobs was setting the pieces of type that made up words. In those days, books and newspapers were printed on presses that used metal type. Every single letter, number, punctuation mark, and space in every line had to be placed in its correct position by hand. This work required great attention to detail, good reading skills, and the ability to work quickly with one's hands.

As Sam set pieces of metal type in trays, he read the stories that they formed. Some stories were about local news; others were about other parts of the country and the world. Setting type helped inspire him to become a writer himself, and he began writing brief sketches for newspapers and magazines long before he was to become "Mark Twain."

Working in printing offices involved much more than reading and writing skills. As an apprentice, or "cub," Sam had to wake up before anyone else, build fires to warm the shop in the winter, go to the town pump to fetch water, sweep out the shop, pick up type off the floor and sort it, clean the printing presses, and fold and deliver the papers. In

Make Printer's Type

Mark Twain's writing career began in the newspaper-printing shops of his hometown when he was a teenager. After training as an apprentice in Hannibal, he worked as a regular, or journeyman, printer in Philadelphia, New York, Washington, and Cincinnati.

This photograph, the earliest known one of Sam, was taken when he was about 15 years old. It was probably taken while he was working in a printing shop, as the strange cap on his head was probably a printer's cap. At first glance, he appears to be holding a brass belt buckle in his hands. He is actually holding a small printer's tray containing the metal letters "S," "A," and "M." He was playing a little joke in the picture.

Anyone who has looked closely at metal type or rubber stamps knows that their lettering is backward on their own surfaces. Why aren't the letters in the photo backward then? The metal letters that Sam is holding in this picture don't appear to be backward because the *whole picture* is actually backward. This photograph wasn't made from an exposed negative, as a modern photograph might be. It is a copy of a tintype—a photograph produced by exposing an image directly onto a metal plate. Because Sam knew how tintypes worked, he also knew that the backward "SAM" he was holding

would read correctly in the finished picture. The image of Sam is, of course, also backward—just as he would have seen himself in a mirror.

You can get a better understanding of how printing with metal type works by making your own block of type out of a raw potato.

WHAT YOU NEED

Adult supervison required

* Kitchen knife
* Several large raw potatoes
* Pencil
* Poster paint
* Wax paper
* Plain paper

With the help of an adult, cut several large, raw potatoes in half, taking care that the cut sides are absolutely flat. Each potato half can be used to make one large letter. Use a pencil to draw the backward outline of a letter on the cut side of a potato half. Do the same on the other halves. Try to make your letters all the same height.

Use a knife to cut along the lines you have marked to a depth of about ½-inch. Then, starting from a point ½-inch down from the outside edge

of the potato half, cut away all the areas that aren't part of the letter you have marked on the surface. Be careful not to cut all the way through your first cut lines.

When your potato letters are ready, spread a thin puddle of poster paint in the middle of a sheet of wax paper. Gently press your potato letters on the paint, one at a time, to cover the surface of each letter. Then firmly press the potatoes on a sheet of plain paper to transfer the characters.

Nineteenth-century printers used hard metal type, which could be reused thousands of times, to print books and newspapers. Unfortunately, your potato type won't last that long! Throw away the potatoes when you've finished this activity.

general, he did all the dirty work and answered everyone else's orders. When he delivered the papers, he had to watch out for dogs, which often bit him.

A Passion for Travel

As Sam's knowledge of the world grew, so did his restlessness. Hannibal had tripled in size while he lived there. Nevertheless, in the early 1850s, it must still have seemed awfully small. It had only 3,000 people—barely enough to fill a single large modern auditorium. Every day, Sam read about the great cities of the East and of Europe, and he watched steamboats landing to unload cargo and take on passengers traveling to faraway places. He dreamed of going somewhere far away to seek adventure and learn about the world.

The passion for travel that Sam felt as a boy would later be expressed in his novels. In *The Adventures of Tom Sawyer*, Tom and his friends are awestruck by the mere sight of a county judge, who comes from a village all of 12 miles away, and who "has seen the world." Tom longs to travel so that he, too, can impress his fellow villagers.

Two things finally happened that convinced Sam that it was time to take off on his own during the summer of 1853, while he was only 17. First, he grew tired of working for his brother's newspaper. Orion—who later regretted the way he had treated Sam—was a domineering boss and didn't approve of many of the things that Sam wrote for his newspaper. Orion was honest and hardworking but was a poor businessman and could never afford to pay Sam wages. Second, an exciting world's fair was going on in New York City at the time, and Sam wanted to see it. In order to get to New York, however, he first needed to save some money. To do that, he decided to go to St. Louis to work as a printer in exchange for real wages.

In June 1853 Sam packed his carpetbag (a simple travel bag made from a piece of folded carpet), said his good-byes, and boarded a steamboat for St. Louis, where his sister, Pamela, lived, 100 miles down the river. Not long after Sam left Hannibal, Orion sold his newspaper and moved north to Iowa, along with his youngest brother, Henry, and their mother.

Although Sam would return to Hannibal a number of times in the future, he would never live there again. Nevertheless, his boyhood life in the town would always remain a happy memory.

2

Life on the Mississippi

Sam was just 17 years old when he left Hannibal in June 1853. That was a young age for a man to be traveling far away on his own, even in those times, when people had to grow up faster than they do now. Missouri was still the gateway to the western frontier, and travel was far from safe or easy. Nevertheless, Sam headed off for St. Louis, where he could make money to finance a trip to New York City.

Growing up in Hannibal, Sam saw steamboats go by almost every day and developed an urge to travel to faraway places himself.

He spent several months living with his sister's family in St. Louis. Two years earlier, Pamela had married William A. Moffett, a successful merchant from Hannibal. Their comfortable St. Louis home would serve as Sam's base through most of the next eight years. It would also be his last home in Missouri.

A great advantage of being a printer in those days was that printers usually had little trouble finding jobs in cities. While Sam lived with Pamela's family, he set type for the St. Louis *Evening News*. His goal was simple: to earn enough money to travel. After about three months, he decided he had saved enough to start moving again. This time he headed for New York City, where the great world's fair at the Crystal Palace had opened in July. Starting north by steamboat and coach, he passed through Chicago, Illinois, and Buffalo, New York, and arrived in New York City in late August. The trip took five days. It was by far the greatest distance Sam had ever been from home.

Life in the Big City

SAM ARRIVED in New York City with a few dollars in his pocket and a $10 bill sewn inside the lining of his coat for safekeeping. The city was unlike any place he had ever seen in his life. With a population of around 600,000 people, it was nearly eight times bigger than St. Louis, and unimaginably larger than Hannibal. One of the earliest preserved samples of Sam's handwriting is a letter he wrote to his sister shortly after arriving in New York. In it, he raved about the marvels of the Crystal Palace, noting that every single day it was visited by more than twice the number of people in all of Hannibal!

Sam soon got a job in a New York printing shop. He rented a room in a mechanics' boardinghouse and settled into a routine of getting up early to go to work. The boardinghouse was the first of many such places in which he would live over the next 17 years. There he took most of his meals in a common dining room. However, he was used to southern foods such as fried chicken, hot biscuits, and cornbread, and he had a difficult time adjusting to northern cuisine. He found other things about living in the North different, too.

The strange sights and smells of the crowded boardinghouses in which he lived joined a growing list of memories that he would later use in his books. In fact, he may have been thinking of his very first boardinghouse experience in New York City when he wrote *The American Claimant* almost 40 years later. That novel vividly describes the impressions of a young Englishman visiting

America, including the first time he answers a boardinghouse dinner bell:

→ *Barrow and Tracy followed the avalanche down through an ever-increasing and ever more and more aggressive stench of bygone cabbage and kindred smells; smells which are to be found nowhere but in a cheap private boarding-house; smells which once encountered can never be forgotten; smells which encountered generations later are instantly recognizable, but never recognizable with pleasure.* ←

This description makes it easy to imagine what Sam experienced the first time he went to dinner in a boardinghouse. Like the fictional Englishman Tracy, Sam felt like he was a foreigner in the North.

Sam earned four dollars a week from his printing job. He looked for inexpensive ways to entertain himself when he wasn't working, so that he could set aside some savings. When he was free during the daytime, he walked a great deal and took in the wondrous sights of America's greatest city. According to letters that he wrote to his mother, he spent his evenings quietly reading at a library for printers that had 4,000 books—more than he had ever before seen in his life.

Sam never intended to stay long in New York, but he had trouble tearing himself away from the city. He grew fond of its special attractions, especially the world's fair. The sheer size of the city amazed him, and he loved to climb to the top of a 280-foot-tall observatory building—an amazing height in those days—and look over the entire city. Even the city's water supply fascinated him. The world's great cities would forever hold a special interest for Sam, and in later years, he would enjoy long stays in many of Europe's biggest cities.

Shortly before Sam left New York, his brother Orion sold his Hannibal newspaper and moved to Muscatine, Iowa, just across the

🐾 Sam at 18.

northern border of Missouri. The move allowed Orion, who was becoming an outspoken abolitionist, to breathe the freer air of a state without slavery. There he bought another small newspaper, the *Muscatine Journal*, and published passionate editorials denouncing slavery. At the time, Sam wasn't completely sure how he felt about slavery himself, but he would eventually share his brother's hatred of it.

The Itinerant Printer

S AM FINALLY LEFT New York in October 1853, and went straight to Philadelphia. There he got another printing job, this time with the *Pennsylvania Inquirer* (now the *Philadelphia Inquirer*). He continued to write letters to his family, and Orion printed many of them in his paper. Sam didn't know it at the time, but writing those letters was training him for the most important career he would eventually have: an author.

After spending about five months in Philadelphia, Sam ventured forth again. He paid his first visit to the nation's capital, Washington, D.C., then revisited New York before returning to the Midwest. By the time he saw his brother and mother again in Muscatine, Iowa, he had spent nearly 15 months on the East Coast. He wasn't yet ready to set-

tle down, however, so he went back to his sister's place in St. Louis and got another printing job. After he got tired of that, he rejoined Orion. His brother was now running a little printing company in Keokuk, an Iowa town located where the Des Moines River joins the Mississippi River.

Sam worked for his brother there for a little over a year, but he again became restless and was itching to get away. Sam's loyalty to his family kept him working for Orion. However, since Orion still couldn't afford to pay him wages, Sam had no money to pay for the traveling he still wanted to do. According to his autobiography, a little miracle saved him from becoming stuck in Iowa. It is a wonderful story, but is also the kind of "Mark Twain" story that we cannot be sure is completely true.

On a bitter-cold and snowy winter day, Sam was walking down Keokuk's deserted main street when the wind blew a $50 bill by him. The bill landed against a wall, and Sam grabbed it. It was the largest sum of money he had ever seen. He assumed that whoever lost the bill would be looking for it, so he advertised his find in newspapers, then waited to see if anyone would claim the money. For several days he suffered horribly, afraid that the owner of the $50 bill would see his advertisement and come and take it away. After four days had passed, Sam could stand the

☞ **Keokuk building (center) in which Orion had his printing office.**

waiting no longer: he decided that the only way to keep the money "safe" would be to leave town with it. He then went by steamboat to Cincinnati, Ohio, where he found yet another printing job and lived in yet another boardinghouse.

Whether or not Sam's story about finding the $50 bill is true, he did go to Cincinnati in October 1856. He was then only about five weeks shy of his 21st birthday. The printing job he had there, for about four months, would be the last one he ever held. However, he would never lose interest in the printing trade.

Letter Writer

SAM SENT LETTERS back to Keokuk, which were published in a newspaper. This time it wasn't Orion's paper to which he was sending his letters, though. For the first time, he was being *paid* by a newspaper publisher for them! That made him a professional writer. He signed the letters with a silly pen name, "Thomas Jefferson Snodgrass," and he deliberately wrote them using poor grammar, errors in spelling, and other such "mistakes." This was a common style among humorous writers at the time. In these letters, which were published in the *Keokuk Post*, he pre-

tended to be a country bumpkin who didn't know how to write any better. For example, this passage describes a train:

→ *When we got to the depo', I went around to git a look at the iron hoss. Thunderation! It wasn't no more like a hoss than a meetin'-house. If I was goin' to describe the animule, I'd say it looked like—well, it looked like—blamed if I know what it looked like, snorting fire and brimstone out of his nostrils, and puffin' out black smoke all 'round, and pantin', and heavin', and swellin', and chawin' up red-hot coals like they was good.* ←

There is a Greek word for that kind of writing: *cacography* (kah-KOHG-rah-fee), which means "bad handwriting" or "bad spelling." In the mid-19th century, many people thought that kind of writing was funny. Now, it is difficult to read it without groaning. Writers who wrote that way also often used odd pen names, similar to Sam's "Snodgrass." Three of the most famous were Artemus Ward, Petroleum V. Nasby, and Q. K. Philander Doesticks. These humorists, and most others of the period, are now almost forgotten, while Mark Twain remains as famous as he ever was.

One reason that people still read Mark Twain's books, and not those of the others, is

Artemus Ward, the most famous humorist in America until Mark Twain came along.

Capture Real Human Speech

Mark Twain had a superb ear for human speech, and his dialogues are often the best parts of his stories. His secret was listening to people carefully and re-creating the language he heard accurately. This extract from a conversation between Huck and Jim in *Adventures of Huckleberry Finn* is an example of "real speech." When Jim asks Huck how much money kings get, Huck answers:

> *"Get?" I says; "why, they get a thousand dollars a month if they want it; they can have just as much as they want; everything belongs to them."*
>
> *"Ain't dat gay? En what dey got to do, Huck?"*
>
> *"They don't do nothing! Why how you talk. They just set around."*
>
> *"No—is dat so?"*

Mark Twain didn't invent language such as that; that was the way that people of Huck's and Jim's social classes actually talked.

WHAT YOU NEED
* Pencil or pen
* Paper

When you are with a group of friends, listen carefully to how each person talks. If you can write down examples of what you hear without attracting attention, do so. Otherwise, wait until you are alone, then try to write down as much as you can remember. Try to notice every sound that people make while talking. Do some people frequently say "um" and "ah"? Do they slip in words such as "like" and "you know"? Your friends don't all talk in the same way. What words, phrases, and verbal mannerisms make each friend's speech unique?

After you have studied conversation for a while, try creating some original dialogue between two imaginary people. In order to test how well you have mastered writing "real speech," set aside your written dialogue for at least a day. When you come back to it later and read it, does it sound natural or artificial? If it doesn't sound natural, try to figure why. Listen to more conversations, and compare what you hear to what you have written. You may be surprised by how much you can discover about the ways people talk.

that the way many other humorists wrote didn't seem natural. It wasn't even the way that ignorant people really talked; it was merely silly. Sam, on the other hand, made his writing seem quite natural and "real," in addition to being very funny. Eventually, though, he settled on a style that combined clearly written prose and correct grammar and spelling with often wild exaggerations and colorful images. This description of a coyote (spelled "cayote" in those days), in the book *Roughing It*, is an example:

→ *The cayote is a long, slim, sick and sorry-looking skeleton, with a gray wolf-skin stretched over it, a tolerably bushy tail that forever sags down with a despairing expression of forsakenness and misery, a furtive and evil eye, and a long, sharp face, with slightly lifted lip and exposed teeth. He has a general slinking expression all over. The cayote is a living, breathing allegory of Want. He is always hungry. He is always poor, out of luck and friendless. The meanest creatures despise him, and even the fleas would desert him for a velocipede. He is so spiritless and cowardly that even while his exposed teeth are pretending a threat, the rest of his face is apologizing for it.* ←

Sam had an especially good ear for human speech, and he wrote colorful dialogue that accurately reflected local dialects and idioms. A wonderful example is a fictional interview, between a Nevada miner named Scotty Briggs and a newly arrived eastern minister, found in *Roughing It*. Briggs wants merely to ask the minister to officiate at the funeral of another miner, but the language each man uses is so different that they can barely understand each other. When Briggs senses that the minister has no idea what he is talking about, he says:

→ *Well, you've ruther got the bulge on me. Or maybe we've both got the bulge, somehow. You don't smoke me and I don't smoke you. You see, one of the boys has passed in his checks and we want to give him a good send-off, and so the thing I'm on now is to roust out somebody to jerk a little chin-music for us and waltz him through handsome.* ←

Alas, the minister only replies,

→ *My friend, I seem to grow more and more bewildered. Your observations are wholly incomprehensible to me. Cannot you simplify them in some way? At first I thought perhaps I understood you, but I grope now. Would it not expedite matters if you restricted yourself to categorical statements of fact unencumbered with obstructing accumulations of metaphor and allegory?* ←

Becoming a Steamboat Pilot

IN FEBRUARY 1857 Sam boarded the steamboat *Paul Jones* and headed down the Ohio and Mississippi Rivers for New Orleans. His later explanation of why he left Cincinnati is as hard to believe as his story about finding the $50 bill that led him there in the first place. When he was 70 years old, he recalled that when he was in Cincinnati he had read a book about the exploration of South America's great Amazon River. He was impressed by what he read about the Amazon's trade in coca—which was believed to have valuable medicinal properties. He decided to go there himself and get rich as a coca trader. With that idea in mind, he took a steamboat to New Orleans, where he expected to catch a ship to Brazil. However, after he reached New Orleans, he learned that, not only were no ships scheduled to leave for Brazil soon, but there probably wouldn't be any ships leaving New Orleans for Brazil *ever*.

> "Be good and you will be lonesome."
>
> —MARK TWAIN

Whatever Sam's real reasons for going to New Orleans were, it was on that trip that he decided to become a steamboat pilot. His interest in piloting went back to his early boyhood in Hannibal. To many small-town folk, steamboats were the most exciting and glamorous things that touched their daily lives. Most boys who grew up in riverfront towns dreamed of becoming steamboatmen. What child wouldn't have dreamed of being part of the crew of a big steamboat sailing off to some distant port? The most important and most glamorous positions on any steamboat crew were those of the pilots—the men who steered the boats and took no orders from anyone, not even their captains.

While steaming down the Mississippi on the *Paul Jones*, Sam became friendly with Horace Bixby, one of its pilots. Bixby was a 30-year-old man with 13 years of experience on the river. He let Sam do some steering, and Sam asked Bixby if he would train him as a pilot. New pilots learned their professions by having licensed pilots take them on as apprentices, or "cubs." Cubs weren't paid while they were training, but they did get cabins and free meals while they were on the boats. After the cubs completed their training—which could take as long as two years—and qualified for licenses, they could expect to make excellent wages.

Bixby accepted Sam as his cub, but only on the condition that Sam pay him five hundred dollars. It was a common arrangement, but five hundred dollars was an impossible sum for Sam to come up with all at once. Bixby agreed to accept one hundred dollars in advance, and to collect the rest after Sam got his license and started earning regular wages. Once their bargain was made, Sam and Bixby returned upriver together, on a steamboat called the *Colonel Crossman*. When they

☛ **Hannibal boys watching steamboats and dreaming of becoming pilots themselves.**

reached St. Louis, Sam borrowed one hundred dollars from his brother-in-law and made his first payment to Bixby.

For the next two years, Sam lived on the river while he learned about steamboating. Boats usually carried two licensed pilots, who took turns at steering in four-hour shifts. Pilots who had apprentices generally let their cubs do most of the steering, while they watched and instructed them. While Sam was cubbing, he had plenty of opportunities to meet and observe other people. What he learned about human nature from the variety of people he saw on steamboats would later help him in his writing. In his book *Life on the Mississippi* he wrote, "When I find a well-drawn character in fiction or biography, I generally take a warm personal interest in him, for the reason that I have known him before— met him on the river."

☛ **Steamboats docked at St. Louis during the 1850s, with an inset photo of Horace Bixby taken in 1907.**

Learning the River

S AM WOULD EVENTUALLY become a fine pilot, but it wasn't an easy trade to learn. Going downriver on the *Paul Jones*, steering down the middle of the Mississippi under Bixby's watchful eye, was fairly easy work. The middle of the river was too deep to present hazards, and, since much of the river is a mile wide, there wasn't much chance of hitting anything or running aground. Steering a boat back upriver, however, was an entirely different matter, as Sam was soon to discover.

Piloting was a highly skilled profession that required a vast amount of knowledge and allowed little room for error. Bixby was a demanding instructor, and Sam was over-

As a cub pilot, Sam didn't think he would ever remember everything he had to learn.

their pilots steered them through the areas where the current moved most slowly—near the river's banks. While the middle of the Mississippi was deep and uncrowded, the water along its banks was shallow and swarming with other boats, as well as underwater hazards such as rocks and tree trunks. Pilots had to be constantly on guard so as not to hit obstructions or run aground.

When Sam signed on with Bixby, he thought that piloting involved little more than steering up and down the center of the river and basking in the glory of being the person in charge. He was astounded to discover that, as a pilot working between St. Louis and New Orleans, he would have to know every feature along every foot of both sides of the river, for a distance of more than 1,200 miles.

Since currents on opposite sides of a river don't behave exactly the same, pilots had to know which side of every stretch offered the fastest sailing. They also had to know where and how to cross over from one side to the other in order to take advantage of the slowest currents available when traveling upriver. Pilots received high wages for a good reason: They were responsible for the safety of their boats and passengers, and their work was extraordinarily difficult.

One of Mark Twain's finest pieces of writing is a series of articles, titled "Old Times on

whelmed by all the details that he had to learn. It didn't take long for him to wonder if he had made a terrible mistake.

The first thing that Sam learned was how different piloting downriver was from piloting upriver. When boats steamed downriver, they were generally steered straight down the center of the river, where the current moved the fastest. However, when they went upriver, the Mississippi," that he published in the *Atlantic Monthly* in 1875, about 14 years after he left the river. He later expanded those articles and made them chapters of his book, *Life on the Mississippi*, which was published in 1883. The "Old Times" articles are a rich memoir of his years as a cub pilot. Like many of Sam's other writings, the articles are a combination of fact and fiction. For example, the cub pilot of the articles seems much younger than the 21-year-old Sam Clemens who became a cub in 1857. Also, the "Mr. B——" of the articles seems much older and sterner than the real, 30-year-old Horace Bixby. Nevertheless, the articles give a rich and essentially accurate account of what Sam went through to become a pilot, and they bring to life a colorful era that disappeared long ago.

Sam was a pilot during a golden age of steamboating on the Mississippi—what he later called its "flush times." It was, however, an age that didn't last long. The first steamboat to travel on the Mississippi came from Pittsburgh, on the Ohio River, and traveled to New Orleans in 1811. As steamboats changed and became more efficient river vessels, a revolution occurred in Mississippi Valley transportation. For the first time, it became practical to transport building materials and supplies of every kind deep into the center of

☞ Snags in the river.

Make a Paddlewheel Boat

Before the invention of steam engines in the late 18th century, the only methods of moving boats up rivers—other than by sail, which was rarely practical on rivers—were by rowing or poling. Going downriver was always easy, and the Mississippi River quickly became the highway for the movement of products—particularly timber—from the Midwest to the Gulf of Mexico. Large quantities of goods could be piled on rafts and simply floated down the river to New Orleans. Getting the rafts back upriver, however, required more effort than they were worth, so they were sold and dismantled for their timber.

The invention of the steam engine revolutionized river transportation by making it possible to move large cargo- and passenger-carrying boats at good speeds against the current. By the 1830s a large number of steam-powered boats, or "steamboats," were moving up and down the Mississippi River, helping to create new towns and settlements.

Because boats traveling on rivers constantly had to float on shallow water, their construction differed greatly from seagoing ships, which were also becoming steam-powered around the same time. Steamboats had flat bottoms, which wouldn't get stuck in shallow water. Seagoing ships had deep keels and were propelled by rotating screws with propeller-like blades that cut deep in the water. Steamboats, on the other hand, were propelled by great paddlewheels, which looked a lot like ferris wheels. The paddlewheels were mostly above water, and then cut just deeply enough into the water to push the boats along—very much like the wheels of a car on solid ground. There were two kinds of paddlewheel boats: sternwheelers, which had single, broad wheels on their sterns, and sidewheelers, which had narrower wheels on both sides of the boats. Sidewheelers were more popular and could be turned more easily, because their wheels could turn in opposite directions.

WHAT YOU NEED

Adult supervision recommended

* Pencil
* Stiff foamboard (available in any art-supply store and in many drugstores)
* Scissors
* Rubber band that fits loosely over the width of the boat
* Swimming pool or tub of water

Use a pencil to trace the main deck and paddlewheel blades of your boat on the foamboard, as shown in the diagram. Use scissors to cut out each piece.

Stretch the rubber band across the rear of the deck, so that the notches hold it in place.

Slide the two paddlewheel blades together, as shown in the diagram. Slip the paddlewheel between the two strands of the rubber band, so that the band holds it in place, and center it. Twist the paddlewheel and rubber band around 5 to 10 times, so that when the rubber band unwinds, the top of the paddlewheel will move forward. Hold the wheel in place with you fingers until you are ready to place the boat in water.

Place the boat in a shallow pool of water (a bathtub is a good place) and release the wheel. The turning wheel will push the boat forward the same way that a real steamboat paddlewheel moves a boat.

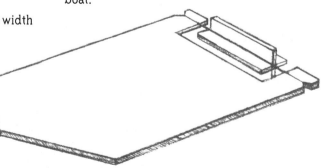

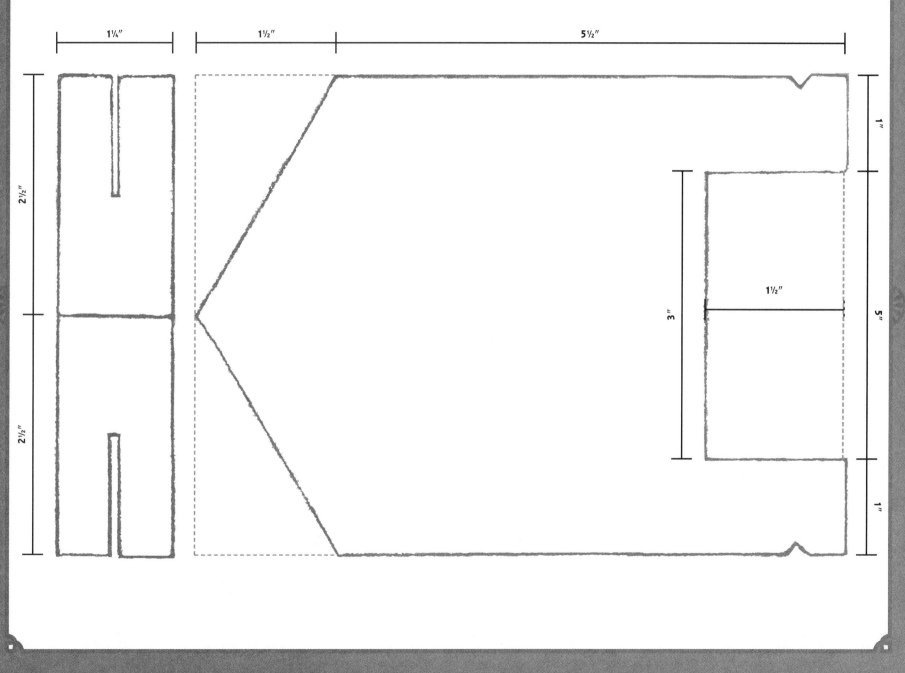

> **"When angry, count four; when very angry, swear."**
>
> — MARK TWAIN

the growing United States. Every year, tens of thousands of migrants to the West made major parts of their journeys on steamboats.

By the time Sam's family was living in Missouri in the mid-1830s, more than 200 steamboats were regularly working up and down the Mississippi River, carrying ever more passengers and cargo. That number doubled each decade, until nearly a thousand boats were on the river in the late 1850s. When the Clemenses lived in Hannibal, their homes were usually within direct sight of the boats on river.

Many years after Sam had achieved his boyhood dream of piloting, he looked back on his steamboating days and fondly recalled the power and independence he had enjoyed as a pilot. Pilots ruled their steamboats from prominent, glass-enclosed pilothouses perched atop the highest decks. When each voyage began, the captain would issue a few instructions for the trip to his pilot. However, once a boat pulled out into the river, its captain's reign was over, and the pilot at the wheel took charge. He could then do whatever he wanted with the boat. No one could tell him what course to follow, how fast to go, or whether to stop or start. He wouldn't want to hear suggestions, even from his own captain, while the boat was underway. Under the laws governing steamboats on the Mississippi, the pilot was regarded as the only person fit to make deci-

sions about its handling. Sam later called the steamboat pilot of his day a true "king . . . an absolute monarch who was absolute in sober truth and not by a fiction of words." The idea of a person exercising such real power is one that always interested him.

Sam very much enjoyed the great respect and courtesy that pilots were shown by their captains and other officers. A crew's respect for its pilots rubbed off on the passengers. For a person who loved being the center of attention as much as Sam Clemens did, it is difficult to imagine a more satisfying occupation than steamboat pilot. Pilots, he said, "were about the only people I ever knew who failed to show, in some degree, embarrassment in the presence of travelling foreign princes." In later years, he would have many opportunities to test that idea, as he was destined to meet presidents, princes, kings, and emperors himself.

Before Sam was to reach the lofty status of a full-fledged pilot of imposing dignity, however, he had a great deal to learn about the river. During his first days as a cub, Bixby constantly rattled off names of islands, bends, and various other landmarks that they passed as they sailed upriver. One landmark looked pretty much like another to Sam, who listened to everything Bixby said with amused indifference. It never occurred to him that he was expected to remember such strange details.

Soon, however, Bixby started asking him to repeat what he had been told.

When Sam couldn't answer a single one of Bixby's questions, Bixby called him "the stupidest dunderhead I ever saw or ever heard of, so help me Moses! The idea of you being a pilot—*you*! Why, you don't know enough to pilot a cow down a lane." He asked Sam why he thought he had told him names of points along the river. Sam could only reply, "Well—to—to—be entertaining, I thought." That merely made Bixby angrier.

After Bixby calmed down, he told Sam to get a little notebook and write down everything he was told. Bixby wasn't cruel, but he was a tough teacher. He understood that Sam would never learn what he had to know unless he was pushed hard. Sam got a notebook and did what Bixby suggested. In fact, that book started him on a lifelong habit of keeping journals—most of which still exist today.

Sam later recalled that his notebook "bristled with the names of towns, 'points,' bars, islands, bends, reaches, etc., but the information was to be found only in the notebook—none of it was in my head." He also noticed another alarming problem: he and Bixby were in the pilothouse only half the time the boat was moving. He was therefore seeing only half the river as they went upstream. To make things even worse, he discovered that, going downstream, nothing looked the same as it had when they were going upstream. It was as though he had to learn two completely different rivers.

Sam also made other alarming discoveries. At midnight during his first night out, he was rudely awakened by someone holding a lantern over his head, telling him it was "time to turn out." He angrily told the man to leave him alone so he could get back to sleep. A few

Horace Bixby teaches Sam the river.

minutes later, however, Bixby arrived, and Sam was soon rushing up the pilothouse steps, carrying in his arms the clothes he hadn't yet managed to put on.

Having to get up in the middle of the night to pilot the boat was something that hadn't occurred to Sam in all the years he had dreamed about being a pilot. He had known that boats kept running through the night, but he had never considered that people had to get out their warm beds to run them. There was

" COME ! TURN OUT ! "

more to being a pilot than romance. It involved real work.

It was probably steering boats on dark nights that made Sam realize how important it was to know the shape of the river intimately. The many twists and bends of the Lower Mississippi formed patterns that guided the pilots. Even if the pilots couldn't see all the landmarks that were visible during the day, they could usually tell where they were by the turns they had to make during the night.

Sam saw an impressive display of piloting skills on one of his first nights on duty. The captain asked Bixby to make an unscheduled stop at a certain farm that ran along the river. When Bixby asked the captain which end of the farm he should stop at, Sam thought that Bixby must be joking. It was a pitch-black night, and it seemed impossible that they would even find the farm, let alone choose at which end to stop. However, to Sam's astonishment, Bixby stopped the boat at the correct spot on the first attempt. He explained that he didn't have to see the farm to know where it was. He found it by following the shape of the river.

On another occasion, Sam was in the pilothouse when the midnight relief pilot committed the unpardonable sin of arriving 12 minutes late. Bixby was furious. He turned the wheel over to the other pilot and walked out, without saying a word. Sam was shocked that

Bixby didn't even tell the other pilot where they were. Sam thought Bixby was acting irresponsibly. It was an inky black night, and they were in a part of the river that seemed to have no shape that could be read.

Sam stuck around, figuring that the pilot would eventually ask him where they were. The man seemed to be a lunatic, however, because he never asked, so Sam stayed with him all night to keep an eye on things. Early the next morning he awakened, stiff and dry-mouthed, on the pilothouse bench. Bixby was back at the wheel, and nothing appeared to have gone wrong. When Bixby asked Sam what he was doing there, Sam explained that he had stayed to help the relief pilot. Now it was Bixby's turn to be surprised. It astonished him that Sam thought that a pilot who arrived in the middle of a dark night to steer the boat should need to be told where he was.

Sam eventually mastered thousands of facts about the river. However, every time he thought that he had learned all there was to learn and his confidence began to grow, Bixby would introduce new complications that forced him to relearn the whole river. Sam had to learn how to read the river going upstream and downstream, in daylight and in darkness, in high water and in low. And if all that weren't enough, Sam learned that the river itself is constantly changing its shape.

The water that flowed down the Mississippi was always shifting course and eating away at the shorelines. Familiar landmarks sometimes disappeared without warning, and occasionally, the river even washed away whole towns.

The Lower Mississippi—the part south of St. Louis—was constantly changing. The Lower Mississippi was an unusually twisty, winding part of the river whose course was made up of S-shaped curves and long, horseshoe-shaped bends. Every so often, the flowing water took a shortcut across a bend, cut itself a new channel, and left part of its old bed high and dry. Sam discovered that pilots had to stay constantly alert to changes; they could never relax.

Learning the river was demanding work, but a cub pilot's life wasn't without diversions. When Sam wasn't at the wheel on his watch, he was likely to be sleeping or taking it easy somewhere else on the boat. As always, he spent a great part of his time reading.

The steamboats that Sam piloted all ran between New Orleans and St. Louis. Since he had no duties while the boats were laid up in port, he always had at least a few days in each city to enjoy himself. When he was in St. Louis, he stayed with his sister's family. He occasionally saw his mother and friends from Hannibal at his sister's place.

A Narrow Escape

AFTER SAM had been working on the river for about a year, he helped his younger brother, Henry, get an administrative job as a "mud clerk" on the big steamboat *Pennsylva-* *nia*, on which Sam had already made several trips. Being a mud clerk was similar to being a cub pilot. Henry didn't get paid, but he could count on eventually being promoted to a paid job, and perhaps even climbing the ranks to become a senior officer. He was 20 years old, and the job was a good opportunity for him.

Sam was assigned to the *Pennsylvania* while Bixby was up north, piloting boats on the Missouri River. With Bixby gone, Sam cubbed under a middle-aged pilot named William Brown. Brown made a strong impression on Sam, who later described him as a "long, slim, bony, smooth-shaven, horse-faced, ignorant, stingy, malicious, snarling, fault-hunting, mote-magnifying tyrant." Finding fault in everything that Sam did, Brown made his life aboard the *Pennsylvania* miserable. Every time Sam went on duty, he wondered what fresh insults awaited him.

While Sam suffered under Brown's tyranny, another cub pilot, George Ritchie, was working the opposite shift under George Ealer, who was as kind as Brown was mean. Occasionally, when Sam was off duty, he would join Ritchie in the pilothouse, and they took turns pretending to be Brown. At night, Sam got his

☞ **Sam and Henry on the *Pennsylvania*.**

revenge on Brown by going to sleep imagining different ways to kill him.

Brown's fault-finding was tiresome, but Sam put up with it until one day when he went too far. While Brown was on duty at the wheel, the captain sent Henry up to the pilothouse to ask him to stop at a certain place. Brown was hard of hearing, but he refused to admit it, so Henry couldn't be sure that Brown heard him. Brown missed the stop, and the captain came up to inquire about it. Brown said that Henry had never delivered the message. But Sam had watched his brother deliver the message. He knew that Brown was lying.

After the captain left, Sam got into an argument with Brown about the incident, and Brown struck Henry. That did it for Sam. He jumped on Brown, pounded him, and made fun of his ignorance and poor grammar. For five minutes, the two men thrashed about on the pilothouse floor, while the *Pennsylvania* plowed down the river, pilotless. Finally, Brown jumped up and took control of the wheel.

Sam retreated from the pilothouse, and the captain called him into his cabin. Sam figured that his piloting career was over. He had committed the "crime of crimes." Not only had he assaulted a licensed pilot who was on duty, he had also been responsible for letting the steamboat run downriver with no one at the wheel. However, when the captain discovered

☞ Sam and Mr. Brown discuss their differences.

☞ Mr. Brown.

what Sam had done, he was delighted, not angry. It seemed that Brown was no better liked by the captain than he was by anyone else. This incident seems to have been the only serious fight that Sam was ever in. And, as it turned out, it may have saved his life.

After their fight, Sam and Brown couldn't work together, so Sam got off the *Pennsylvania* when it docked in New Orleans. A few days later, in early June 1858, the *Pennsylvania* left for St. Louis. Sam followed in another boat, the *Alfred T. Lacy*. As the *Lacy* sailed up the river, Sam heard disturbing reports of a boiler explosion on the *Pennsylvania*.

Steamboats were fragile crafts, and they were not built to last very long. Collisions and groundings could easily wreck them, and their brittle cast-iron boiler tanks couldn't withstand high temperatures and high pressures forever. The average Mississippi steamboat lasted only five years, and boiler explosions were common.

When the *Pennsylvania's* boilers exploded near Memphis, nearly 150 people, including Brown, were killed. Sam's brother Henry wasn't badly hurt by the explosion, but when he returned to the burning boat to help others, he inhaled boiling hot steam. He and other injured people were taken to Memphis for medical treatment. Sam found Henry in a makeshift hospital there and spent a few days with him before he died.

Afterward, Sam's fellow steamboatmen called him "Lucky" for not having been aboard the *Pennsylvania* when it blew up. Sam always hated that nickname, however, because he felt responsible for his brother's death.

The Licensed Pilot

AFTER TWO YEARS as an apprentice, Sam finally got his pilot's license in May 1859. He spent another two years on the river, but he would write little about that period of his life. *Life on the Mississippi* devotes 17 chapters to his years as a cub, but only one short paragraph to his two years on the river as a licensed pilot. However, those two years were happy ones for him. He worked steadily on steamboats, and he earned himself a good reputation as a pilot.

☞ **The licensed steamboat pilot, at the approximate age of 25.**

Although Sam later described himself as only "a good average St. Louis and New Orleans pilot," he was probably much better than average. He never had a serious accident, and he appears to have been steadily employed—something that wasn't true of all pilots at the time. He made $250 a month—a huge sum at that time, and as much money as the vice president of the United States made. Since he didn't have to pay for room or board while he was on steamboats, his expenses were low. After paying off his debt to Bixby, he was able to send money to his mother and save money for himself. In early 1861 he treated his mother to a steamboat trip to New Orleans. It was the grandest city she had ever seen, and she was terribly proud of her youngest surviving child.

After Sam got his license, his future seemed secure. There weren't many jobs in those days that offered the excitement, prestige, and generous pay that pilots enjoyed. They got to travel almost constantly along a continuously changing river, yet they were rarely away from their homes for more than a week or two at a time. They also got to meet new and interesting people.

However, the same four years that Sam was a pilot were troubled years for the nation, which was tearing itself apart over the issues of slavery and states' rights. The election of

Abraham Lincoln to the presidency in November 1860 increased Southern opposition to the Union. A month later, Southern states began seceding from the Union. Sam's days as a pilot were numbered, for when war came, commercial steamboat traffic on the river ended.

Sam shows his mother the river.

3

Roughing It in the West

On April 9, 1861, Sam celebrated the second anniversary of being a licensed steamboat pilot. He looked forward to a long and rewarding career on the river, but it wasn't to be. Only three days later, rebel troops fired on the Union's Fort Sumter in Charleston, South Carolina. The Civil War was underway, and life on the Mississippi would never be the same again.

The Coming of War

THE NATION was coming apart, and the importance of the Mississippi River put Sam in the middle of the developing conflict. While war fever was growing, he had continued to pilot up and down the river. He had been in New Orleans in January, on the day that Louisiana had seceded from the Union. He was there again three months later, when news that the country was at war arrived from Charleston. Afterward, he made one more trip to New Orleans as a pilot. Sam then found himself out of work. Winning control of the Mississippi was an important part of the Union's plan to split the South. This meant that there would be fighting on the river, and that would make commercial steamboating impossible. The river was big, but not big enough for fragile steamboats to find safety from gunboats and shore batteries.

As the war began, steamboatmen with whom Sam had worked began choosing sides. The last captain under whom he had served took his boat over to the Confederate side. Sam's former teacher Horace Bixby was a New Yorker; he went on to serve the Union Navy with distinction on the river. Sam wanted to get back to Missouri before he made a decision about his position on the war. He was fortunate to secure passage out of New Orleans on one of the last boats back to St. Louis, where he spent several weeks with his sister's family.

When Sam reached Hannibal in June, he found his hometown in turmoil. Union troops were coming, and Missouri's pro-Confederate governor, Claiborne Fox Jackson, called upon men to report for duty with the militia. This was a confusing time in Missouri. While Missouri was a slave state whose culture was tied to the South, most of its white citizens opposed secession. They wanted to stay in the Union. The coming of the railroads was shifting the state's trade from the south to the

The Civil War

FROM EARLY 1861 through early 1865, the United States was torn apart by a war between the Northern states and the Southern states that had left the Union and formed the Confederate States of America. While many of the issues that led to the war were complicated, one central issue stood out: the question of whether individual states had the right to leave the Union. As the war progressed, ending slavery also became an important issue. After the war ended, the passage of the Thirteenth Amendment to the U.S. Constitution abolished human slavery throughout the United States.

Several Southern states, including Missouri, never seceded from the Union and thus were never part of the Confederacy. However, many people in Missouri favored the Confederate cause. Missouri citizens' division of opinion about the Civil War made the state a difficult place for Sam to be in. He liked the idea of going someplace where he wouldn't have to choose sides.

north and the west. In February the governor held a state convention in St. Louis to vote on secession. Missouri's delegates voted to stay in the Union.

Slavery had little to do with pro-Union sentiment in Missouri. In fact, many slave owners wanted to stay in the Union, because they thought it would protect slavery better than the Confederacy would. The Union had strong laws ensuring that slaves who fled from a slave state like Missouri to a free state, such as Illinois, would be returned. If Missouri had joined the Confederacy, it would have been surrounded on three sides by foreign territory, with no chance of getting back slaves who slipped across its borders.

Although Missouri was never part of the Confederacy, many of its people were ready to fight for the South. At the same time, the leaders of the Union Army weren't about to let Missouri slip over to the Confederate side if they could prevent it. Tensions were running high in Missouri when Sam returned home.

Like all other states, Missouri had a tradition of calling up men to serve in its state guard, a militia formed to protect the public safety during emergencies. Governor Jackson had the legal right to call men to report to the state guard, and he did so. What he intended to do with these guardsmen isn't completely clear, but the men who reported had to swear loyalty to the state of Missouri and to the Union. Whatever the men's motives for answering the governor's call to join the militia, they were *not* entering Confederate service.

Sam later wrote that he and several of his old Hannibal friends responded to the governor's call. Except for the fact that they carried real guns (Sam had a squirrel rifle), they were about as much like a military unit as the boys playing army in *The Adventures of Tom Sawyer*. They had no training, they wore their own clothes, and they had no real officers in charge of them. For several weeks, they bored themselves with tedious patrolling near Hannibal.

Union troops took control of Missouri, and they offered amnesty to members of the state guard who laid down their weapons. Sam's little unit, like others, melted away, and that was the end of Sam's military career.

As his friends chose sides in the war, Sam found himself torn between his love of the United States and his feelings for the South. As a man who had lived in the North, he had a broader view of the war than most Southerners. He was growing to love the country as a whole, and he did not want to see it torn apart. Also, as a Missourian, he was a man from a state that was itself torn between the North and the South. He welcomed any opportunity that would take him away from the Civil War and prevent him from having to choose sides.

Opportunity
in the West

SUCH AN OPPORTUNITY came along at the very moment that Sam was looking for a way to escape. As the war began brewing, the Union government separated Nevada from the Utah Territory and made it a new territory of its own. Nevada now needed a government and government officers.

Shortly after being sworn in as president of the United States, Abraham Lincoln appointed Sam's brother, Orion, to be the secretary to the new Nevada Territory. Orion—whose own pro-Union sympathies in the Civil War were never in doubt—had campaigned hard for Lincoln's election, and this appointment was his reward. He got it because of his connections with the St. Louis lawyer Edward Bates, whom Lincoln made his first attorney general. Orion had worked in Bates's law office during the 1840s and had helped him campaign for Lincoln in the 1860 presidential election.

To Orion, the appointment was a godsend. For the first time in his life he had an important and well-paying job. However, he also had a problem. Nevada's capital, Carson City, was more than 1,500 miles away, and he didn't have enough money to get there. Sam, on the other hand, had saved a great deal of money from his piloting work. Since he happened to be looking for someplace to go, he offered to pay Orion's way to Nevada. In return, Orion agreed to make him his private secretary.

☛ Dreaming of riches and adventure in the West.

Sam had other reasons for going west. He thirsted for travel and adventure, and a trip to the remote "Wild West" of cowboys, outlaws, and Indians promised plenty of both. Moreover, he had long been smitten by "gold fever," and he hoped to strike it rich in Nevada's fabulous silver and gold mines. When the California gold rush had started in 1849, gold fever swept through Missouri, and thousands of treasure seekers passed through the state on their way west. Many of them went through Hannibal. Some of Sam's neighbors headed west to look for gold. In fact, his good friend John Robards had gone to California with his father when he was only 12 years old. The image of John's leaving for California burned into Sam's memory:

→ *I remember the departure of the cavalcade when it spurred westward. We were all there to see and to envy. And I can still see that proud little chap sailing by on a great horse, with his long locks streaming out behind. We were all on hand to gaze and envy when he returned, two years later, in unimaginable glory— for he had traveled. None of us had ever been forty miles from home. But he had crossed the continent. He had been in the gold mines, that fairyland of our imagination.* ←

The Big Muddy

CONTRARY TO MANY PEOPLE'S BELIEFS, the "Big Muddy" is not a nickname for the Mississippi River, but for the Missouri River. Much of the Mississippi is indeed muddy, but the Missouri River is even muddier. The Missouri is also actually longer than the Mississippi—about 2,540 miles, compared to the Mississippi's 2,340 miles. Its headwaters are in the Rocky Mountains near the spot where Idaho, Montana, and Colorado meet. It feeds into the Mississippi just north of St. Louis, making it possible, during certain times of the year, to take a boat from Montana more than 4,000 miles down to the Gulf of Mexico.

Now it was Sam's turn to go west and look for that fairyland of his boyhood imagination. He would not find much gold there, but what he did find proved to be even more valuable.

After meeting up in Keokuk, Sam and Orion went down the Mississippi River to St. Louis to say their farewells to their mother and sister, and to prepare for their long journey. There they took passage on the steamboat *Sioux City* up the muddy Missouri River to St. Joseph. Sam was impressed by how much the Missouri differed from the Mississippi. It was narrower, shallower, muddier, and full of dangerous snags.

Sam enjoyed riding on the top of the stagecoach during the morning runs.

The Journey West

LOCATED NEAR the northwestern corner of Missouri, St. Joseph was the starting point for overland journeys to the West Coast. Wagon trains were organized and provisioned there, and cross-country stagecoaches took on passengers there. Using money he had saved from his piloting income, Sam bought seats for himself and his brother on a stagecoach going to Carson City, Nevada. The one-way fare for each of them was $150—as much as a month's wages from Orion's new job. On July 26, 1861, the brothers piled into a stagecoach pulled by teams of 16 horses and began a 1,700-mile journey that would last for 19 days.

Except for a two-day layover in Salt Lake City, Utah, their stagecoach stopped only to change teams and drivers and to let passengers eat and refresh themselves. The passengers slept inside the coach's cabin, which Sam and Orion shared with a constantly changing assortment of other passengers and big bags of mail.

From St. Joseph, the stagecoach passed through a corner of Kansas, across southern Nebraska and a corner of Colorado to Wyoming, then down through northern Utah and across central Nevada. The moment they entered Nebraska, they left the United States and were in the "territories"—the lands owned by the United States that were not yet states.

Sam and Orion happened to make their trip during the brief period when the pony express system was used to carry mail between St. Joseph and California. To deliver a single bag of mail, as many as 20 men using as many as 150 horses, one man riding at a time, covered 2,000 miles in only eight days. That speed may not seem fast now, but it was three times faster than the speed of stagecoaches. It was also a very expensive way to send letters. The pony express began in early 1860 but disappeared the following year after the completion of the first transcontinental telegraph line, which offered a much faster way to send long-distance messages.

While Sam and Orion traveled on their stagecoach, they saw some pony-express riders. A passage in *Roughing It* describes the excitement felt by the stagecoach passengers the first time a pony-express rider passed them during daylight:

→ *Every neck is stretched further, and every eye strained wider. Away across the endless dead level of the prairie a black speck appears against the sky, and it is plain that it moves. . . . In a second or two it becomes a horse and rider, rising and falling, rising and falling—sweeping toward us nearer and nearer—growing more and more distinct, more and more sharply defined—nearer and still nearer, and the flutter of the hoofs comes faintly to the ear—another instant a whoop and a hurrah from our upper deck, a wave of the rider's hand, but no reply, and man and horse burst past our excited faces, and go winging away like a belated fragment of a storm! ↩*

Although traveling in a cramped stagecoach and bouncing along on rough roads for nearly three weeks was exhausting, Sam enjoyed the journey, and he was fascinated by all the new sights he encountered: the wide open plains of Nebraska, the rugged Rocky Mountains, and the desolate deserts of Utah and Nevada. He was especially impressed by the sight of men cutting blocks of pure ice out of the ground in the Rocky Mountains, in the midst of sweltering hot August days—an impossibility at lower altitudes.

The prospect of seeing real Indians and desperadoes also excited Sam, and he soon saw both. During a stop in southeastern Wyoming, he and Orion had breakfast with a notorious outlaw named Jack Slade, who was then working for the Overland stagecoach line. At the time, Sam didn't know about Slade's reputation for killing people, but his description of meeting the man, in the book *Roughing It*, makes it sound as though he had been afraid that Slade might kill him after regretting giving him the last cup of coffee in the breakfast pot. A few years later, Montana vigilantes hanged Slade because of his drunken shooting sprees.

Sam and Orion finally arrived in Carson City, Nevada, in the middle of August. Dusty and rumpled from their long trip, they couldn't have made much of an impression when they tumbled out of their stagecoach. However, Carson City didn't look like much, either. Its population of 2,000 people made it even smaller than Hannibal. It was a flat, dry, and windswept place, and most of its buildings were little more than wood shacks. In fact, it had so few buildings that finding office space for the new government that Orion had to organize was a serious problem.

☛ **Sam nervously refuses Slade's offer of the last cup of coffee at breakfast.**

Orion Clemens and Nevada

NEVADA FIRST CAME under American control in 1848, after the United States won the Mexican War and took possession of California and most of what is now the American Southwest. Except for California, which became a U.S. state rather quickly, the new lands were divided into "territories," each of which was administered by officials appointed in Washington, D.C. Through the 1850s, Nevada was a part of the new Utah Territory, and it attracted little outside attention. However, things changed dramatically after 1858, when silver and gold were discovered in western Nevada. When it became clear that the region had some of the world's richest deposits of precious metals, prospectors poured in, and towns, such as Virginia City, rose up.

Nevada's mineral wealth made it vitally important to the Union government as the Civil War approached. In March 1861 President James Buchanan signed a law making Nevada a separate territory, which now needed its own government. After Abraham Lincoln became president that same month, he named James W. Nye Nevada's first governor and gave the job of secretary of state to Orion Clemens. For three years, Orion played a major role in organizing the Nevada Territory's new government and served as acting governor during Nye's frequent absences.

Nevada was rushed into statehood in late 1864. Had Orion stayed there, he might have become an important figure in state government. However, he missed his chance. He served briefly in the new legislature, but ended up going back to the Midwest. He never held another important government position.

☞ **Orion Clemens.**

Life in Nevada

THE FIRST PLACE in which Sam and Orion lived in Nevada was a boardinghouse run by an Irish woman. Most of her boarders were rough young men who had come west in the hope of making their fortunes in the new gold and silver mines. They didn't expect much in the way of luxuries. The sleeping area they shared was similar to that of army barracks, except that the boarders used sheets as "walls," in order to have a little privacy.

Sam went to Nevada with the idea of working as Orion's private secretary, but Orion never had much for Sam to do and little extra money to pay him. However, this wasn't like the old days, when Sam had done printing work for Orion without pay. Now they were in a new country—one in which riches seemed to lie just around the corner. Sam soon struck off on his own. He still had some of his savings, and he was anxious to see the new country and to look around for opportunities to get rich.

One of Sam's first Nevada adventures was a hike into the nearby Sierra Nevada with a man named John Kinney. They walked to Lake Tahoe (then called Lake Bigler), which is on the border between Nevada and California. Lake Tahoe is the largest freshwater lake in the western United States and is 6,225 feet above sea level. The combination of the lake's size and the thin mountain air make for magnificent scenery. The lake itself has unusually clear water, even now.

Using a boat that they found at the lake, Sam and John enjoyed lazy days of fishing and basking in the sun. Sam especially liked to drift on the lake's surface, hanging his head over the edge of the boat and staring at the bottom of the lake. The water was so clear and bright that, even at depths of over 100 feet, he could easily see fish swimming on the bottom.

While Sam and John were camping out at Lake Tahoe, they got the idea of staking a timber claim along its shoreline. They figured they could make big money selling trees to Nevada's mines, which always needed wood to prop up their deep underground tunnels. Laws for timber claims were similar to those for mining claims. Anyone claiming a piece of timberland had to do some real work on the claim to make it valid. For Sam and John, this meant fencing in the area they claimed and building a house on it. They started chopping down trees to make a building, but it wasn't long before they tired of the effort. It was too much like real work. The log house they'd planned to build ended up a shack made out of brush.

Sam and John's brush house was so flimsy that it wouldn't have satisfied the least picky of the three little pigs. It didn't satisfy Sam and John, either; they continued to sleep outside in the open air even after it was finished. One day their campfire got out of control and set the forest on fire. They ran to a safe location and watched as flames raced up trees that were more than 100 feet tall. The fire destroyed their entire claim. That was the end of their brush house—and of their dreams of getting rich on timber.

☛ Sam and John's brush house.

Prospecting for Silver and Gold

S AM'S NEXT GET-RICH-QUICK SCHEME was prospecting for gold and silver. Real fortunes were being made in western Nevada when he got there, and the territory buzzed with rumors of ever-richer finds being made. The most exciting rumors came out of the Humboldt region, about 125 miles northeast of Carson City. When Sam heard that Humboldt might be the richest gold and silver field in the world, he caught the prospecting fever.

The following December, Sam joined an expedition to Humboldt with three other men. They took a horse-drawn wagon that was loaded with provisions but ended up walking the whole distance. In fact, their wagon was so heavy and their horses were so feeble that they had to help push the wagon themselves. Their 11-day journey across a frigid wasteland was exhausting, but they were excited about the wealth they expected to find.

Like Sam's timber-claim adventure, the Humboldt trip was a bust, and not a pleasant one. Sam thought that all he had to do to find gold and silver was walk around and scoop up nuggets from the ground. The first night he was in Humboldt, he left the camp by himself and went around collecting all the glittering rocks he could find. Feeling proud of himself, he came back to the camp with his collection, expecting his partners to jump with joy. Instead, Cornsburg Tillou, the most experienced member of the group, told him that all his samples were worthless iron pyrite, "fool's gold." Sam learned that, not only was it true that "all that glitters is not gold," but that *nothing* that glitters is gold. It was a lesson he would have done well to remember.

After several backbreaking weeks of staking claims, digging, and blasting, Sam and his

☛ Fool's gold!

partners decided to give up and go back to Carson City. By then the winter weather was becoming harsh. One night the men got hopelessly lost in a blizzard. They huddled together all night, thinking they would never see the morning. When the new day dawned, they discovered that they were only 15 steps away from a warm stagecoach station.

The disappointing trip to Humboldt knocked some of the enthusiasm out of Sam, but he wasn't yet ready to give up on prospecting. His next venture took him southwest, to the booming Esmeralda mining district. He had visited that region the previous fall to buy mining claims for himself and Orion. In February 1862 he returned to Esmeralda's chief mining camp, Aurora, and settled in to do some serious work on his claims. Aurora was a true boomtown, and Sam had only to look around to see that many men really were getting rich off their claims.

Over the next seven months, Sam shared a rough cabin with a slightly older man named Calvin Higbie, who had studied civil engineering and had had some mining experience in California before coming to Nevada. Sam and Cal had some wonderful adventures together, but Sam's luck in Esmeralda was ultimately no better than it had been in Humboldt. By then, his savings were almost gone, and he had to write to Orion frequently for

Aurora

NOT MANY TOWNS in the United States have histories as strange as that of Aurora. When Sam Clemens prospected there in 1862, he thought he was living in California. So did most Aurora residents. After all, Aurora was then the official seat, or capital, of California's Mono County. However, the border between Nevada and California hadn't yet been thoroughly surveyed, and Nevada claimed the district, too. Nevada and California almost went to war over the disputed border. Orion Clemens happened to be Nevada's acting governor when the dispute was at its hottest, and he resolved the crisis peacefully. After a proper survey of the border was made, Aurora was found to be inside Nevada after all. California's Mono County then moved its seat to Bridgeport, and Aurora became the seat of Nevada's Esmeralda County. When Esmeralda's mining boom petered out, Aurora became a ghost town, and Esmeralda County moved its seat to Goldfield. Aurora itself ended up in Mineral County.

How many American towns can claim to have been in three different counties and two different states?

money to buy supplies and more claims. Digging tunnels and holes was exhausting, and it wasn't the kind of work that got easier as failures piled up.

Eventually, Sam and Cal both ran out of money. They wondered how they would even pay for food. When things became desperate, Sam took a job for a salary of $10 a week plus board. The job was in a quartz mill—a place where ore that had been dug up by miners was

crushed so that its gold and silver could be extracted. Sam's job was to scoop sand through a screen with a long-handled shovel. Now, this really was *work*, and Sam wasn't good at it. Most of the sand he tried to toss up through a screen simply went over his head and fell down inside the back of his clothes. After only one week, he was ready to quit, but before he could, he was fired.

Despite their disappointments and setbacks, all wasn't drudgery for Sam and Cal. They took time out from prospecting to go sightseeing. Their expeditions took them as far as California's Yosemite Valley, where they marveled at the spectacular scenery, which few people had ever seen before. They also spent a week camping out at California's strange Mono Lake, located 15 miles south of Aurora.

Because of its extremely high salt content, the water of Mono Lake is not only undrinkable, it is dangerous to swim in. Sam's amusing exaggerations of the lake's dangers in *Roughing It* make the book's chapters about the lake fun to read. However, the same chapters also offer vivid and accurate descriptions of the lake that are frequently quoted by modern environmentalists working to protect Mono Lake from destruction.

Sam and Cal actually did come close to scoring a big success once, but, through carelessness, they ended up with nothing. Cal became interested in something odd about the ore being extracted from a rich mine called the Wild West. With Sam's help, he sneaked down the Wild West's main mine shaft one night and found something that confirmed his suspicion: A rich vein of ore that wasn't part of the Wild West claim was running diagonally through the Wild West's ore vein. It was what miners called a "blind lead." Since Cal and Sam were the only people who knew of the blind lead's existence, they had the right to stake their own claim to it and open a new mine.

Roughing It gives such an extravagant account of the "blind lead" episode that it reads like complete fiction. However, the essence of the story is true. Cal and Sam did file a claim for the blind lead, and they would have become rich if they had held onto it. However, to make their claim stick, they had to do some work on it within 10 days. Unfortunately, Cal wandered off on a wild goose chase after a fabled gold mine, and Sam went off to help nurse a sick friend. Since neither of them told the other what he was doing, neither did any work on the claim. They both returned to Aurora and found that other miners now owned their claim.

That was probably as close as Sam ever got to realizing his dream of quick riches. However, we can be glad that he blew that chance. Had the blind lead made him rich, he might never have become an author.

Becoming a Newspaperman

DESPITE THE RIGORS of mining camp life, Sam found enough leisure time to go back to writing letters to newspapers. He sent several to the Keokuk *Gate City* that described the mining camps of Nevada. He wasn't paid to write these letters; he wrote them for his own enjoyment. Some of his letters found their way back to Nevada when people in Keokuk sent them to Orion. Orion, in turn, showed the letters to the editor of the Virginia City *Territorial Enterprise*, Nevada's leading newspaper. The editor liked what he read, and he printed one of Sam's letters in his own paper. Sam then sent more letters directly to the *Territorial Enterprise*. He was glad to see them published, but he didn't think enough of them to put his own name on them. Instead, he signed them "Josh"—a word that means about the same thing as "joke."

Sam wrote the Josh letters mostly to amuse himself. He didn't expect to make money from them, and he certainly didn't expect them to make him famous. His Josh letters didn't make him a nationally known figure, but they did start him in that direction. In August 1862 the owners of the *Territorial Enterprise* invited Sam to come up to Virginia City and become

☞ **Virginia City, Nevada.**

a reporter, at a salary of $25 a week. This wasn't much compared to what Sam had made as a steamboat pilot, but compared to what he had been making in Esmeralda, it was big money. Equally important, writing for a newspaper was a lot more pleasant than digging and blasting.

Sam wrapped up his belongings in a bundle and set off on foot for Virginia City. After walking more than 100 miles through the wilderness, he presented himself at the *Territorial Enterprise* office. He must have been quite a sight! Unshaven and covered with dirt from his trek, he was wearing a slouch hat, baggy clothes, and a Navy revolver. According to legend, he strode right into the newspaper office, sat down at a desk, and immediately started writing.

While a great many things went into the creation of "Mark Twain," the role of the *Territorial Enterprise* in Sam's career cannot be overstated. During the decade before he arrived in Virginia City, Sam had done a fair amount of writing for various newspapers and magazines. However, it wasn't until he settled into his new job with this newspaper that writing became his full-time trade. Now he began to think of himself as a professional writer. What he learned from writing articles almost every single day would affect how he wrote through the rest of his life.

Virginia City was an extraordinary place when Sam arrived there, and the *Territorial Enterprise* was an extraordinary newspaper.

Virginia City was one of the greatest boomtowns of the West. Built on the slopes of Mount Davidson, about 12 miles northeast of Carson City, the town arose after the discovery of the fabulous Comstock Lode in the late 1850s. By the time Sam arrived there in September 1862, the town had a lively population of more than 10,000 people and was booming with the excitement generated by the mineral riches being dug out of the tunnels deep below it. Vast fortunes were being made, and almost everyone in the town was prospering, including the owners of the *Territorial Enterprise*.

The newspaper was owned by two men who were both about Sam's age. Dennis McCarthy and Joe Goodman each had excellent business sense and an appreciation for creative writing. In an age long before movies, television, and radio were invented, newspapers played a more vital role in American life, and even a town the size of Virginia City could support more than one daily paper. The *Territorial Enterprise* was the most important paper in Virginia City and one of the most influential papers along the entire Pacific Coast. Everything it printed was sure to be read throughout both Nevada and California.

Sam's job was to write daily articles on every kind of event that was of interest to local residents, from developments in the mines to business affairs to school reports—even to

Joe Goodman.

shoot-outs in the streets, which weren't rare occurrences. His reporting work took him to every corner of the region and introduced him to everyone of any consequence. As he had done while piloting on the Mississippi, he made a close study of the various people he met, and he added those observations to his store, which he would later draw on as a writer.

One of the most remarkable things about the owners of the *Territorial Enterprise* was their willingness to let their writers have fun. When it was important for the paper to get the facts straight, it got them straight. At other times, however, reporters could write almost anything they wanted, whether it was true or not. The important thing was to make the paper interesting enough so that people would want to read it. That policy suited Sam just fine. He was never above exaggerating facts and even writing outright lies about people whom everyone in town knew. Most of the paper's readers understood that they shouldn't take everything he said seriously, but occasionally Sam's carelessness with the facts got him into trouble.

Sam's worst trouble came when he wrote a completely fictitious story about a massacre, in which a man killed six of his children and scalped his wife. Every person who knew the place where the massacre supposedly occurred

should have instantly figured out that the story was fake. Its geographical facts were all nonsense. The story also contained an outright impossibility: it said that the murderer rode all the way to Carson City after cutting his own throat "from ear to ear," then fell dead in front of a saloon. No one with a slit throat would live long enough to get on a horse, let alone ride any distance.

Despite the obvious absurdities in the story, many readers believed it, and other newspapers in Nevada and California reprinted it as if it were real news. When the truth came out, many people were outraged and called for Sam's head. Feeling ashamed of himself because of the trouble his story was causing his employers, Sam offered to resign. But Joe Goodman refused to accept his resignation. He told Sam that the fuss would soon blow over, and that the incident would actually help his reputation in the long run. Goodman was right.

The freedom that Sam enjoyed in writing for the *Territorial Enterprise*, and the wild and exciting events going on around him, helped to develop his creativity. It is difficult to imagine how he would have become as skilled and popular a writer as he eventually would be had he never worked as a reporter in Virginia City.

Toward the end of 1862, Sam added a new assignment to his reporting duties: covering sessions of the territorial legislature in nearby

☛ **The bloody murderer rides into town.**

Unmask a Hoax

Early in Sam's writing career in Nevada, he became famous for publishing hoaxes—deliberately false stories that he wrote mostly for fun. He wanted readers to believe outrageous lies, while at the same time giving readers clues that his stories were fake. One of his most famous hoaxes was about a "petrified man"—a Nevada Indian who had, supposedly, been turned to stone by natural geological forces.

A petrified man was found some time ago in the mountains south of Gravelly Ford. Every limb and feature of the stony mummy was perfect, not even excepting the left leg, which has evidently been a wooden one during the lifetime of the owner—which lifetime, by the way, came to a close about a century ago, in the opinion of a savan [an expert] who has examined the defunct. The body was in a sitting posture, and leaning against a huge mass of croppings; the attitude was pensive, the right thumb resting against the side of the nose; the left thumb partially supported the chin, the fore-finger pressing the inner corner of the left eye and drawing it partly open; the right eye was closed, and the fingers of the right hand spread apart. This strange freak of nature created a profound sensation in the vicinity, and our informant states that by request, Justice Sewell or Sowell, of Humboldt City, at once proceeded to the spot and held an inquest on the body. The verdict of the jury was that "deceased came to his death from protracted exposure," etc. The people of the neighborhood volunteered to bury the poor unfortunate, and were even anxious to do so; but it was discovered, when they attempted to remove him, that the water which had dripped upon him for ages from the crag above, had coursed down his back and deposited a limestone sediment under him which had glued him to the bed rock upon which he sat. . . .

Now, how can we tell that this story is a hoax?

Read Sam's story carefully and list every detail that appears to be unlikely or impossible. The geographical details are important, but you don't need to understand them to detect the hoax. (Hint: Have someone sit on a stool—or do it yourself in front of a mirror—and duplicate every detail of the petrified man's posture.)

After you figure out Sam's clue that this is a hoax, write one of your own. Remember these rules: The story must be fiction, but written as if it were fact, and it should contain clues that show it to be false.

ANSWERS

1. The Indian was supposed to have been dead for 100 years. No 18th-century Nevada Indian could have had a wooden leg.

2. It would have taken far longer than a century for the Indian's body to turn to stone.

3. The description of the Indian's pose indicates that he is thumbing his nose and winking—clear proof that Sam was merely having fun.

Carson City. While in Carson City, he stayed with Orion, whose wife and daughter had come out from Iowa to join him. Now one of the most powerful figures in Nevada, Orion owned a fine two-story house, which he had built for his family. During Governor Nye's frequent—and occasionally long—absences from the territory, Orion served as acting governor. His home thus became one of the most important social centers in Nevada. His wife, Mollie, loved acting as the territory's "first lady."

Becoming "Mark Twain"

IN FEBRUARY 1863, while he was in Carson City covering the legislature, Sam decided to start signing his reports to the *Territorial Enterprise* with a new pen name: Mark Twain. Before then, he hadn't signed his articles at all. Now that he was becoming an important journalist in Nevada, he wanted readers to know who was writing his articles. Using pen names was common among reporters and other writers in those days. For example, before Sam came along, the *Territorial Enterprise*'s best-known writer was William Wright, who called himself Dan De Quille—a pun for "dandy quill," which meant "good writer."

Orion's Carson City house—in which Sam first used the name "Mark Twain"—as it looks today.

"Mark Twain" not only sounded like a real name, it also had a special meaning. In the language of Mississippi steamboatmen, it stood for a depth of two fathoms, or 12 feet. On the river, two fathoms was generally regarded as the dividing line between water that was dangerously shallow and water that was sufficiently deep to be safe for a steamboat to pass through. Sam was intimately familiar with the words; every time he'd heard "by the mark twain!" called out when he was piloting, he knew that the water's depth had changed.

Make a Miniature Lead Line

In navigation, "mark twain" means "mark two," or the second mark on lead lines, which have been used since ancient Egyptian times to measure depth in rivers and shallow inland waterways. A lead line is long rope with a heavy lead weight attached to one end. Colored markers are tied at different spots on the line to represent different depths. As a boat or ship moves along, a crewman stands as close to the water line as possible and, using a softball pitcher's underhand delivery, swings the weight around in big circles to build up momentum, then lets it go into the water in front of him. As the boat moves forward, the weight pulls the line down to the bottom of the waterway, and the man reads the depth off the marker closest to the surface. Each "mark" represents one fathom, which is equal to six feet. "Mark twain" means a depth of 12 feet—the dividing line between safe and dangerous depths on a river.

☛ **Casting a lead line.**

WHAT YOU NEED
* 5-ounce lead fishing weight (or something similar in weight and size)
* At least 6 feet of strong cord or string
* Ruler or tape measure
* Felt-tip pen
* Scissors
* Small scraps of brown, white, and red cloth

A real lead line is at least 20 fathoms, or 120 feet, long. Instead of feet, we'll use inches here, so each of our "fathoms" will be only 6 inches long instead of 6 feet long. Also, we'll make only a half-length lead line, which will be 60 inches, or 5 feet long.

Tie the fishing weight to one end of the cord. Measuring up from the weight, use the ruler and the pen to mark the cord at these lengths:

- 2 **"fathoms"** (12 inches);
- 3 **"fathoms"** (18 inches);
- 5 **"fathoms"** (30 inches);
- 7 **"fathoms"** (42 inches);
- 10 **"fathoms"** (60 inches).

Cut strips from each scrap of cloth—6 brown strips, 1 white strip, and 1 red strip—each about ½-inch wide and 3 inches long. The brown strips will represent leather.

Tie 2 brown strips at the "2-fathom" mark, 3 brown strips at the "3-fathom" mark, the white strip at the "5-fathom" mark, the red strip at the "7-fathom" mark, and 1 brown strip at the "10-fathom" mark. (Make sure that the brown strips are tied as shown in the picture.) Cut a small hole in the middle of the strip that is tied at the "10-fathom" mark.

You now have a miniature lead line that will work like a real one in shallow water. If you want to try casting it, do it outdoors; make sure that the lead weight is tied securely to the cord or string, and that you are not near anyone or anything that you might hit.

Sam's pen name would become one of the most famous of all time. From that moment until the end of his life, he would sign "Mark Twain" to almost everything he published. However, he never stopped using his real name, Sam Clemens, and he never hid the fact that Mark Twain and Sam Clemens were the same person.

Moving to San Francisco

IN THE SPRING OF 1864, Sam again found himself in trouble because of something that he wrote. This time the trouble was more serious. While acting as chief editor during Joe Goodman's absence, he got into a nasty argument with the editor of a rival newspaper, and he published a letter to the man, in which he challenged the editor to a duel. Challenging people to duels was something that a lot of people on the frontier did in those days. However, most duels never actually took place, and Sam certainly didn't expect this one to. Surprisingly, the editor accepted his challenge. He was ready to fight! With the help of Steve Gillis, a friend who worked as a printer for the newspaper, Sam managed to get his rival to withdraw from the duel. However, because a new federal law made dueling a crime, Sam worried that he might be in trouble for even suggesting the duel. He decided it would be wise to get out of the territory.

By then, Sam had visited San Francisco several times and had grown to like that booming city on the Pacific Coast. In May, he and Gillis got on a stagecoach and left Virginia City for California.

Like Virginia City, San Francisco was a mining boomtown—but on a much bigger scale. Spanish missionaries had founded the city in 1776—the year of America's Declaration of Independence—and it had remained little more than a sleepy village until 1848. In that year, gold was discovered in northern California, and the United States took over the state after winning the Mexican War. Soon a great gold rush began, and San Francisco blossomed into a real city. California's population grew so rapidly that its statehood was granted only two years after gold was discovered.

By the early 1860s, San Francisco had a population of more than 100,000 people, and its great, well-protected bay was one of the busiest ports in the United States. There, Sam found numerous daily newspapers, real opera houses, fine hotels and restaurants, and many other big-city attractions, as well as beautiful natural surroundings. San Francisco was an exciting place to be.

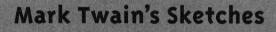

Mark Twain's Sketches

EARLY IN HIS WRITING CAREER, Sam's favorite form was the sketch. Sketches are similar to short stories or essays. Usually built around a single idea, they don't have developed characters, and they often have little plot. Sam's first book, *The Celebrated Jumping Frog of Calaveras County, and Other Sketches* (1867), was a small collection of his early sketches.

Sam wrote a number of funny sketches that are still read and enjoyed today. In "Aurelia's Unfortunate Young Man," for example, Sam pretended to be giving advice to a young woman whose fiancé is having accident after accident. The man is losing body parts so fast that the woman is afraid that by the time she marries him, there won't be much left of him!

☞ **Aurelia's unfortunate young man.**

Although he still held a large amount of mining stock (which he had collected through purchases and gifts in Nevada), Sam needed cash right away. Within a few weeks of arriving in San Francisco, he got a job as a reporter for the *Morning Call*, one of the city's several daily newspapers. Steve Gillis went to work for the paper as a printer. Over the next several months, Sam and Steve roomed together in San Francisco, moving to a new boarding-house almost every month.

The *Morning Call* was the smallest daily in the city, and Sam was its only full-time reporter. He was what was known as a "beat" reporter. Every day he had to tramp around the city looking for news. Long visits to the court-house to see what crimes had been committed and who was being convicted became a regular part of his routine. Unlike Virginia City's *Territorial Enterprise*, the *Morning Call* was a sober-minded publication with no sense of humor. The dull routine of reporting work soon wore on Sam.

Sam also resented restrictions on what the paper would print. After he saw several policemen mistreat a Chinese man, he wrote a scathing story about police misconduct. The paper never printed it because it didn't want to offend its readers, few of whom cared what happened to Chinese people. Eventually, Sam began neglecting his duties. After only four months, he was fired. That was the last regular newspaper reporting job he ever had. Things weren't grim, however. Sam made a deal with Joe Goodman to write daily letters from San Francisco for the *Territorial Enterprise*.

Meanwhile, Sam was becoming interested in more creative forms of writing. He continued to read a great deal, as always, and he began contributing humorous articles to local literary magazines. Although San Francisco was a young city, it had a lively cultural life and was home to many fine writers, such as Joaquin Miller, Ambrose Bierce, and Bret Harte, who also edited a literary magazine to which Sam contributed. Sam and San Francisco were a perfect match.

Sam also wrote several memorable stories about the bad things that can happen to children who behave properly, and the good things that can happen to children who behave badly. Especially funny are his sketches that offer such questionable advice to children as:

→ *If your mother tells you to do a thing, it is wrong to reply that you won't. It is better and more becoming to intimate that you will do as she bids you, and then afterward act quietly in the matter according to the dictates of your best judgment.* ←

→ *Good little boys must never tell lies when the truth will answer just as well. In fact, real good little boys will never tell lies at all—not at all—except in case of the most urgent necessity.* ←

→ *You ought never to knock your little sisters down with a club. It is better to use a cat, which is soft. In doing this you must be careful to take the cat by the tail in such a manner that she cannot scratch you.* ←

Trouble with the Police

BY THE END OF 1864, Sam was again in trouble. This time it was for publishing a newspaper article attacking police corruption. Once again, it was time for him to get out of town. It happened that his friend Steve Gillis was also in trouble with the police—for fighting with a man who turned out to be the police chief's pal. Sam and Steve went east to an isolated mining camp in Tuolumne County, California, where two of Steve's brothers and their partner, Dick Stoker, were prospecting. They all lived in a rough log cabin, in a place with the unforgettable name of Jackass Hill.

After more than two years of working as a reporter, Sam was back to living the life of a prospector. This time, however, he wasn't quite so concerned about getting rich. It was just as well, as Jackass Hill was no Virginia City. In fact, it was about as quiet and remote a place as could be found in California. For several months, Sam merely dabbled in prospecting, using the local "pocket-mining" technique—which involved finding little deposits of gold near the surface of the ground. He also spent time reading, taking it easy, and enjoying the agreeable company of the Gillis brothers and Dick Stoker.

Stoker was one of the great storytellers of the Old West. Sam would later use the stories he heard from Stoker in his own books. The most famous of these is a hilarious tale about a bluejay, which Sam included in his book *A Tramp Abroad*. Stoker is referred to in that book as "Jim Baker," a "middle-aged, simple-hearted miner" who had spent years living in a lonely corner of California, studying the ways of animals and learning to understand their languages. Baker declares that among all the birds and beasts, the best talkers are bluejays. He goes on to tell about a bluejay that once mistook the hole in the roof of a house for hole in a tree and tried to fill it with acorns.

After a few weeks at Jackass Hill, Sam and one of the Gillis brothers went up into Calaveras County, to try their luck at prospecting there. They didn't fare much better than they had in Tuolumne, but Sam struck a different kind of gold. It was one of those little, apparently inconsequential things that people sometimes do that change their lives.

While Sam was in Calaveras County's Angel's Camp, it rained a great deal, and he decided that sitting in a saloon there was more agreeable than working outside during a downpour. He particularly enjoyed the company of the local bartender, a former Illinois River steamboat pilot named Ben Coon. Like Dick Stoker, Coon was a good storyteller.

Among other tales, he told Sam a peculiar story about a frog.

What most amused Sam about Coon's story was not its content, but the manner in which Coon told it—in a deadpan fashion in which he seemed unaware that he saw anything especially funny or remarkable about what he was telling. According to Sam:

→ *He never smiled, he never frowned, he never changed his voice from the gentle-flowing key to which he tuned his initial sentence, he never betrayed the slightest suspicion of enthusiasm; but all through the interminable narrative there ran a vein of impressive earnestness and sincerity, which showed me plainly that, so far from his imagining that there was anything ridiculous or funny about his story, he regarded it as a really important matter.* ←

The story—as Sam later retold it—is about an Angel's Camp man named Jim Smiley, who loved to bet on anything and everything. He most enjoyed betting on a frog that he had trained to jump farther than any other frog in the county. One day, a stranger came into Angel's Camp and said he wanted to bet against Smiley's frog. Since he didn't have a frog of his own, Smiley left to find one for him.

After Smiley returned with another frog, the men laid down their wagers. The stranger's frog jumped well, but Smiley's frog wouldn't jump at all. Smiley thought that his frog looked lumpy and baggy. He picked it up and said, "Why, blame my cats if he don't weigh five pounds!" He turned the frog upside down, and it belched out two handfuls of lead shot. The man had fed Smiley's frog lead pellets to weigh him down! Smiley took off after the stranger, but it was too late to catch him.

After spending a few weeks at Angel's Camp, Sam and Steve Gillis quietly returned to San Francisco, where Sam took a room in the Gillis family rooming house. Back in the city, Sam wrote up Ben Coon's jumping frog story, adding many details and twists of his own. On the suggestion of the popular humorist Artemus Ward, whom he had met in Virginia City, he sent the story to a publisher in New York who was preparing a book that Ward had worked on. Since it was too late to get Sam's story into the book, the publisher gave it to a magazine. This proved to be a lucky break. If the story had been published in Ward's book, it would probably have died in obscurity. Instead, it was reprinted in magazines and newspapers all over the United States, and "The Celebrated Jumping Frog of Calaveras County" helped spread the fame of the name Mark Twain.

The year 1865 was a comparatively quiet one for Sam. He continued to write sketches, but he probably worked less that year than at almost any time in his life. In October 1865 a big earthquake hit San Francisco. It was an exciting event, and Sam, who was lucky not to have been injured during the quake, wrote numerous amusing anecdotes about it, which would be included in his book *Roughing It*. One of the anecdotes includes this description of a minister conducting a church service:

→ *The first shock brought down two or three huge organ-pipes in one of the churches. The minister, with uplifted hands, was just closing the services. He glanced up, hesitated, and said: "However, we will omit the benediction!" — and the next instant there was a vacancy in the atmosphere where he had stood.* ←

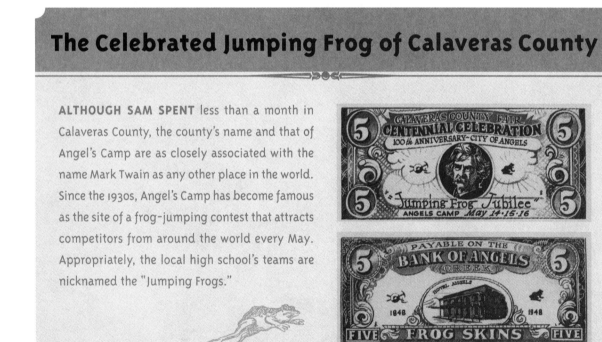

The Celebrated Jumping Frog of Calaveras County

ALTHOUGH SAM SPENT less than a month in Calaveras County, the county's name and that of Angel's Camp are as closely associated with the name Mark Twain as any other place in the world. Since the 1930s, Angel's Camp has become famous as the site of a frog-jumping contest that attracts competitors from around the world every May. Appropriately, the local high school's teams are nicknamed the "Jumping Frogs."

Off to Hawaii

THE FOLLOWING YEAR, Sam grew restless, and he cast about for something new to do. He had been offered a chance to sail to the Hawaiian Islands on a new steamship called the *Ajax*, but had turned it down. Afterward, he regretted passing up the trip, and he persuaded a Sacramento, California, newspaper, the *Sacramento Union*, to send him to Hawaii to report on the sugar industry, which was of great interest to people on the mainland.

In March 1866 he sailed on the *Ajax* to Honolulu, Hawaii's capital city. It was Sam's first real sea voyage. He planned to spend about a month on the islands, but he enjoyed himself so much there that he ended up staying for four months. Everything about the islands—from their spectacular natural beauty to their violent history to their unusual government—fascinated him. At that time, Hawaii was a foreign country known to Americans as the Sandwich Islands.

Sam explored the largest islands and sent his reports back to the *Sacramento Union* in 25 long letters. After he returned to California, he wanted to use those letters for a book on Hawaii, but he never got around to writing it. However, he did include some of the letters in *Roughing It*, and all of his original letters were published after he died. Meanwhile, the

The Sandwich Islands

DURING THE 19TH CENTURY, Europeans and Americans called Hawaii the "Sandwich Islands." It seems an odd name, but it had nothing directly to do with the "sandwiches" that people eat. In 1778 British explorer Captain James Cook was the first European to visit the islands, and he decided to name them after his friend and patron John Montague, the fourth earl of Sandwich. However, no one asked the Hawaiians themselves for their opinions on the new name, and they continued to call their home the kingdom of Hawaii. After Cook's visit, European diseases almost wiped out the islanders. Nevertheless, when Sam visited in 1866, Hawaii was still an independent kingdom.

publication of his letters in the *Sacramento Union*, as well as in other newspapers, which reprinted them, added still further to his growing reputation.

The months that Sam spent on the islands were unlike anything that he could have imagined before he went there. The spectacular tropical scenery alone was like nothing he had ever seen. He was so taken by the beauty of the rainbows that he saw every day—sometimes even at night—that he thought it was a pity that Cook hadn't called Hawaii the "Rainbow Islands." He hiked and rode horses throughout the largest islands, and he explored the craters of giant volcanoes. He even tried to surf—

something that few Americans of his time had even *heard* of, let alone tried.

Sam met King Kamehameha V and other members of Hawaii's royal family and developed a strong interest in the islands' government. The kingdom had its roots in ancient Polynesian culture, but its also adopted western institutions, which resembled those of Great Britain's parliamentary government. The combination was a strange mix of cultures, and it seemed especially strange to Sam because the country itself was so puny.

With only about 60,000 subjects (about a fifth of the number of Hawaiians who lived there during Captain Cook's time), King Kamehameha ruled over the equivalent of about half the number of people living in San Francisco. Nevertheless, the kingdom boasted many of the features of modern European nations: a royal family, a legislature, titled government ministers, fancy palace officers, army generals, and other officers—some of whom were Americans and Europeans. On top of all this, the government was visited by envoys and ambassadors from the United States and other nations. Sam thought it all added up to a great deal more grandeur than was needed and called Hawaii "a play-house 'kingdom.'"

Although Sam never wrote a book on Hawaii as he'd planned, his experiences there gave him the germ of an idea for a novel that he did eventually write: *A Connecticut Yankee in King Arthur's Court*. Nineteenth-century Hawaii was a long way from the sixth-century England in which *A Connecticut Yankee in King Arthur's Court* is set, but the combination of modern and feudal government institutions that Sam saw in Hawaii

👉 Wipe out.

gave him the idea of humorously exploring contrasts between ancient and modern practices. In *A Connecticut Yankee in King Arthur's Court*, a 19th-century American travels back in time to King Arthur's days in England and tries to modernize the country.

Sam wrote serious pieces during this time, too. While he was in Hawaii, he wrote a story about the survivors of a clipper ship that had sunk. The *Sacramento Union* was the first to publish a report on the disaster, and the article added to Sam's fame.

In July 1866 Sam said goodbye to Hawaii and boarded the clipper ship *Smyrniote* for San Francisco. The voyage gave him a firsthand appreciation of the difference between sailing and steam-powered ships, as the trip home took more than twice as long as the trip to Hawaii on the *Ajax* had taken. For several days, the *Smyrniote* was caught in dead-calm waters and didn't move an inch. This would be Sam's last long voyage on a sailing ship, but in later years, he would write dream stories about people traveling on sailing ships that find themselves becalmed in strange places.

When Sam finally reached San Francisco, he discovered that his stories from Hawaii had made him a celebrity. He soon did what many famous people of his time did: arrange to give a lecture. Public lectures were an important part of 19th-century American culture. In an age without radio, television, or movies, virtually all public entertainments were live. These included stage plays, musical concerts, reviews, and lectures. Organized lecture tours became a big business after the Civil War, and some people made good incomes traveling from town to town delivering lectures on subjects of popular interest.

Sam returned from Hawaii a recognized authority on the Sandwich Islands, and he arranged to give a lecture on that subject. He booked a large music hall for an evening early in October and had posters printed. The posters promised that his lecture would provide information on the "absurd customs and characteristics of the natives" of the Sandwich Islands and a description of Hawaii's great Kilauea volcano. It ended with a line that would later become famous:

Doors open at 7 o'clock
The trouble begins at 8 o'clock.

As the lecture date approached, Sam began to lose his nerve. He wondered what he would do if no one came. Even worse, suppose no one who did come laughed at his jokes? Sam's lecture seemed funny to him at first, but as he worked on it, it seemed horribly dreary, and not a bit funny at all. He thought of dragging a coffin onto the stage and turning his

Stage fright.

lecture into a funeral. Panic-stricken, he begged friends to come and laugh loudly when he signaled to them. As the big day approached, he couldn't eat or sleep.

The day of the lecture finally arrived. Sam went to the music hall in the afternoon to see how ticket sales were doing. Finding the box office closed, he guessed that his fears had been correct. No one was buying any tickets. He then sneaked into the building through a back entrance, walked out on the hall's stage, and gazed out over the empty seats. His gloom was now complete. Few people can have been as certain that they were about to fail as Sam was at that moment. He hid in the back of the theater and awaited his fate.

After a few hours he returned to the stage to meet his doom. To his astonishment, he found all of the seats in the theater filled with people with friendly, expectant faces. For several minutes he was paralyzed by stage fright, and he wasn't sure he could even speak. Afterward, he remembered that moment as being worse than even the worst seasickness. After he got past that feeling, however, he was fine. Sam would never again experience stage fright.

The audience ate up Sam's Sandwich Islands lecture, in which he mixed interesting and important facts with wild exaggerations and humor. Typical of the exaggerations in both his travel books and his lectures is his description of Hawaiians—whom he called "Kanakas":

→ *It is said by some, and believed, that Kanakas won't lie, but I know they* will *lie—lie like auctioneers—lie like lawyers—lie like patent-medicine advertisements—they will* almost *lie like newspaper men. They will lie for a dollar when they could get a dollar and a half for telling the truth.* ←

The booming success of his lecture made Sam realize that he now had a new way to make his living: by talking. His success in San Francisco was the first of many hundreds of lectures that he would eventually give. Less than two weeks after his San Francisco triumph, he set off on a brief lecture tour of northern California and western Nevada. Everywhere he went, people roared with delight and left feeling not only that they had been well entertained, but also that they had learned something.

The lecture tour allowed Sam to return to Virginia City as a hero, but the pleasure of seeing his old friends again was slightly spoiled by an incident that occurred after he lectured in Gold Hill, a town next to Virginia City. While Sam and his manager were walking back to Virginia City in the dark, they were held up by several masked and armed men who took all their valuables. Afterward, Sam learned that the whole thing had been a practical joke; the armed desperadoes were actually several old friends. But he was not amused. Sam always hated practical jokes.

With a profitable lecture tour behind him and his newfound celebrity, Sam decided that he had achieved all the success that the West had to offer him. It was time to return home and try to make a name for himself in the East. He was especially eager to see New York City again. He made arrangements to serve as a paid correspondent in the East for San Francisco's *Alta California* newspaper. Instead of traveling by stagecoach, as he had done on his voyage west, he chose to return by a sea route that would take him through Central America. Fifteen days after his 31st birthday, he boarded the steamship *America* to begin a new phase in his life.

An unwelcome practical joke.

4

Becoming an Author

California's gold rush had transformed San Francisco from a sleepy Mexican village into a booming American city, and people now looked for a faster way to cross the continent. When Sam and Orion went west in 1861, stagecoaches offered the fastest transportation available. However, the coaches still took a long time and were too expensive to move great numbers of people. Transcontinental

railroads were on the way, but the first one would not be completed until 1869.

Meanwhile, there was another way to travel between California and the East: by ship. Before the mid-19th century, most people traveling from the East to the West Coast by ship went all the way around South America's Cape Horn—a long and often dangerous voyage. The great number of prospectors and immigrants that flooded into California after 1849 prompted the development of a much shorter route across Central America. Of course, the ships themselves could not cross Central America until the Panama Canal opened in 1914. Meanwhile, a land route across the isthmus, or narrow neck of land, was in development.

The *America*, the ship on which Sam sailed out of San Francisco on December 15, 1866, anchored off the coast of Nicaragua 14 days later. Following what was by then a well-traveled route, Sam and 400 other passengers then crossed Nicaragua. They went first by wagon, then by a steamer on Lake Nicaragua, and finally by a steamboat down a river to the Caribbean coast. There they boarded the steamship *San Francisco* and continued their voyage to New York. The entire trip, including a two-night layover in Nicaragua, took only 29 days—about the same length of time that an overland stagecoach trip across North America would have taken. And the trip was a lot more comfortable and less expensive.

Sam enjoyed the trip, especially the scenic beauty of Nicaragua. He also gained something valuable that he would later use in his books: a wonderfully colorful character in an old sea captain. During his voyage down the Pacific Coast, he became a friend of Ned Wakeman, the captain of the *America*. Wakeman was a salty old sailor who had spent most of his life at sea. He had educated himself, mainly by studying the Bible, about which he loved to talk. In Captain Wakeman, Sam knew he had found a rare treasure.

Sam later transformed Wakeman into the unforgettable Captain Ned Blakely in *Roughing It*. In *The American Claimant* Wakeman appears as the kind-hearted Bible misquoter Captain Saltmarsh. Sam also used Wakeman in several other stories, but nowhere more memorably than in *Extract from Captain Stormfield's Visit to Heaven*, which he published the year before he died. When Sam first met Wakeman, the captain told him about a strange dream he had had in which he went to heaven. Sam was so taken by Wakeman's ideas about heaven that he spent nearly 40 years toying with a story based on Wakeman's dream before he finally published part of it.

Meanwhile, after arriving in New York, Sam had to figure out what to do next. His dream of striking it rich as a miner had evaporated, but now he saw the possibility of making his living as a journalist and a lecturer. However, he still wanted to travel to far-off lands. He especially wanted to go to Asia and even around the world. To do that, he needed to find a newspaper that would pay his way.

Sam decided to go home to the Midwest and see his family and old friends before he set off on his next foreign adventure. Although he didn't return as a rich prospector, he was definitely a success, and he could be proud of what he had accomplished. Before he left New York, he arranged for the publication of his first book. This was a collection of short stories and sketches titled *The Celebrated Jumping Frog of Calaveras County and Other Sketches*.

Sam returned to Missouri in early March after a nearly six-year absence. He visited his mother and sister in St. Louis, then went up to Hannibal and Keokuk. In those and other river towns, he delivered his Sandwich Islands lecture to appreciative audiences. He must

"A man should not be without morals . . . it is better to have bad morals than none at all."

—MARK TWAIN

have been pleased to know that old friends and neighbors had to pay good money to hear him talk.

On his second pass through St. Louis, he met the future explorer Henry M. Stanley, with whom he began a lifelong friendship. A journalist himself, Stanley covered Sam's lecture for a local newspaper. A few years later, he would become famous when a New York newspaper sent him to East Africa to search for the Scottish missionary-explorer David Livingstone. Several more expeditions to Africa would add to Stanley's fame.

A New Kind of Travel

IT WAS AROUND THIS TIME that a new idea for travel came into Sam's head. He read that Henry Ward Beecher, a famous Protestant minister in Brooklyn, New York, was planning a sightseeing cruise to Europe and the Holy Land, on a ship named the *Quaker City*. The cruise attracted a great deal of attention. In those days, most people who crossed the Atlantic did so for practical reasons, such as emigration or business. The idea of going that far merely to do some sightseeing was new, and the idea of a ship crossing the Atlantic solely for that purpose was unheard of. It was another example of the great changes taking place in transportation, and Sam wanted to get in on the cruise.

In early 1867 Sam was still writing travel letters from the East to the *Alta California* in San Francisco. He convinced that newspaper's editors that they should send him on the *Quaker City* expedition as their correspondent. The editors agreed to pay the $1,250 fee for his passage, as well as $20 each for 50 long letters that he promised to write for them during the trip. Sam then returned to New York City and booked his passage on the *Quaker City*.

While he waited for the cruise to begin, Sam enlisted the help of Frank Fuller, a New York businessman whom he had met in Utah, to arrange to deliver his Sandwich Islands lecture in several places in New York City. At Fuller's suggestion, he scheduled his first lecture in the city's largest auditorium, the Cooper Union. Sam protested that it was far too big a hall to fill, but Fuller confidently predicted success and promised to pay all of the expenses himself if the lecture lost money.

As had happened in San Francisco, Sam became nervous as the lecture approached. Tickets weren't selling, and he dreaded the embarrassment of facing thousands of empty seats. Finally, he begged Fuller to distribute free tickets so the hall at least would not be empty. Fuller gave away tickets, and 2,000 people jammed into Cooper Union. Every seat was filled, and some people even sat on the stage behind Sam while he spoke. His lecture was another smashing success, and it received fine reviews in the papers. A week later, his first book came off the presses. Sam was now both a celebrated lecturer and a published author.

Write a Travel Letter

Mark Twain won his first truly widespread fame for the travel letters he wrote on the *Quaker City* voyage. His letters mixed humor with detailed facts in ways that make the subjects jump to life and stick in readers' minds. Try your hand at writing a memorable travel letter of your own.

WHAT YOU NEED
* Pencil or pen
* Paper

Think about writing a letter to an imaginary newspaper, as if the letter will be published.

In it, you will describe a place that you have visited recently. Before you start your letter, list all the things about the place that make it important, interesting, or fun. Where is the place? How many people live there? What special attractions (like tall mountains or great buildings) does it have? Do the people who live there have customs or habits that differ from what you're used to? Do they talk differently? Is the food different?

Write your letter, discussing the most interesting points that you have listed. Be as creative—and funny—as possible.

The *Quaker City* Cruise

ON JUNE 8 Sam boarded the *Quaker City* and prepared to steam out of New York Harbor. Several celebrity figures had been expected to be passengers, including Reverend Henry Ward Beecher and General William T. Sherman, a top Union Army commander during the Civil War. As it turned out, Beecher decided not to make the voyage, and Sherman's War Department duties kept him from making the trip. Sam suddenly found that *he* was the big "celebrity" on the cruise, and he was given the large cabin that had been reserved for Sherman.

Because of the cruise's original connections with Beecher's Protestant congregation, many passengers thought that the voyage's main purpose was educational. They saw it as a kind of Christian pilgrimage to the Bible lands. Most passengers were older than Sam, and many had a pious attitude toward religion that he didn't share. However, there were enough young men of a different frame of mind onboard to ensure that Sam would have good company throughout the trip. He quickly fell in with a group of fellow passengers who would rather play cards than attend prayer meetings.

The *Quaker City* voyage lasted just over five months. The ship traveled from New York to the Azores Islands, about 800 miles west of Portugal, and to the Mediterranean Sea. It stopped in France, Italy, Greece, and Turkey before entering the Black Sea and the Crimea, which was then part of Russia. After returning to the Mediterranean, the ship stopped at the locations we now know as Lebanon, Israel, and Egypt, then sped back to New York.

The *Quaker City* voyage is famous because of the long book that Sam wrote after the trip: *The Innocents Abroad, or The New Pilgrims' Progress*. He drew heavily on the travel letters he had written for the *Alta California* to write the book, but he also made many changes to the writing he'd done in the letters. The book is a mostly accurate account of the voyage. Like *Roughing It*, however, *The Innocents Abroad* should not be read as a completely true history.

The Innocents Abroad is fun to read. Sam filled it with humorous characters and incidents, as well as vivid descriptions of real places. For example, the book explains how narrow Jerusalem's ancient streets were by describing cats jumping across them, from one rooftop to another. A chapter on Egypt contains an unforgettable description of young local hustlers dragging Sam and his companions up the side of the Great Pyramid:

☛ **At sea on the *Quaker City*.**

Climbing the Great Pyramid.

→ *Each step being full as high as a dinner-table; there being very, very many of the steps; an Arab having hold of each of our arms and springing upward from step to step and snatching us with them, forcing us to lift our feet as high as our breasts every time, and do it rapidly and keep it up till we were ready to faint . . . I beseeched the varlets not to twist all my joints asunder; I iterated, reiterated, even swore to them that I did not wish to beat any body to the top; did all I could to convince them that if I got there the last of all I would feel blessed above men and grateful to them forever. . . .* ←

One of Sam's goals regarding both his travel letters and *The Innocents Abroad* was to poke holes in romantic American ideas about Europe and the Holy Land. Almost everywhere he went, he refused to be awed by things he'd been taught as a child to revere. He poked fun at local legends, dubious religious relics, famous paintings, and romantic travel books that described beauty and charm where it did not exist. He was particularly scathing in his descriptions of the Holy Land, which he found a hot, impoverished, and dreary region with no charm whatever.

Sam also had fun writing about his *Quaker City* shipmates. Indeed, *The Innocents Abroad* contains almost as much writing about them as it does about the places Sam visited. He was particularly critical of his fellow passengers' tendencies to collect souvenirs wherever they went, even if it meant chipping pieces off ancient walls and statues. He understood that if every person who visited a place like Athens's incomparable Parthenon took away a single little piece, eventually there would be nothing left. What the relic collectors did was simply vandalism. After the trip was over, he would develop a successful lecture on the subject, which he would call "The American Vandal Abroad."

Americans who read Sam's travel letters— and later, his book—were sometimes shocked by his views, but they also found his opinions refreshing. Used to hearing about the superiority of European culture, American readers welcomed Sam's radically different take on the subject, especially as it was spiced with so much humor.

During the *Quaker City*'s longer stops, Sam spent a considerable amount of time ashore. He saw a great deal of France, Italy, and the Holy Land, and he participated in many exciting and amusing adventures. For example, when the ship stopped at Greece, local officials permitted no one to go ashore because of a health quarantine. But that didn't stop Sam and several other men. After dark, they slipped ashore and sneaked into Athens. *The Innocents Abroad* has a marvelous description of their midnight visit to the Parthenon.

Through the Holy Land

THE HIGHLIGHT of Sam's entire trip was a two-and-a-half week overland expedition through the Holy Land—the biblical region in which Christ had lived. The journey took Sam and several other men through what are now Lebanon, Syria, Israel, and Palestine. In 1867 the entire region was under the rule of the

Mark Twain and the Czar

THE *QUAKER CITY* stopped at Yalta, a city in the Crimea. Russia's ruler, Czar Alexander II, happened to be staying at his summer palace nearby, and he invited the Americans to visit him. The United States had recently purchased Alaska from Russia, and American feelings toward Russia were especially friendly at the time. Sam had the distinction of writing the brief speech that the American consul read to the czar in everyone's presence.

☛ **Sneaking through Athens at night.**

Turkish Ottoman Empire. When the *Quaker City* landed at Beirut, the travelers hired a local guide to lead them overland to Jerusalem. The guide assembled a lavish outfit for them, complete with horses, pack animals, and comfortable tents. The expedition took the travelers to such famous Bible sites as Dan, Bethlehem, Nazareth, the Sea of Galilee, the Dead Sea, and Jerusalem.

Sam was so busy with activities on the ship and sightseeing ashore during the voyage that it is difficult to understand how he found time to write more than 50 travel letters, each of which was about 2,000 words in length. The letters are packed with facts on local history and geography; he must have spent a great deal of time reading to gather all that information. He loved to read about history, however, and must have had a good time putting his letters together.

Long before the *Quaker City* excursion ended, Sam's letters began appearing in the *Alta California* and other newspapers across the United States. More than anything else he had done up to that time, the writing of those letters made the name Mark Twain famous. When he returned to New York in November, Sam really was a celebrity. Within a few days of his arrival, a book publisher named Elisha Bliss asked him to write a book on the *Quaker City* excursion.

Meanwhile, Sam needed wage-paying employment, a job that would leave him plenty of time to write the book. He soon found one: Nevada's new senator, William M. Stewart, hired him to serve as his private secretary. Sam had known Stewart earlier in

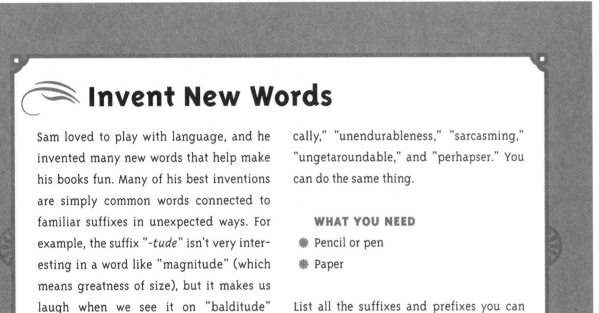

Invent New Words

Sam loved to play with language, and he invented many new words that help make his books fun. Many of his best inventions are simply common words connected to familiar suffixes in unexpected ways. For example, the suffix "-*tude*" isn't very interesting in a word like "magnitude" (which means greatness of size), but it makes us laugh when we see it on "balditude" because we expect to see "baldness."

Sam got great mileage out of such simple suffixes as "-*ing*," "-*ly*," "-*ness*," "-*able*," and even "-*er*" in invented combinations such as "circusing," "Christian-Scientifically," "unendurableness," "sarcasming," "ungetaroundable," and "perhapser." You can do the same thing.

WHAT YOU NEED
* Pencil or pen
* Paper

List all the suffixes and prefixes you can think of and try attaching them to words they usually don't go with. See if you can come up with some interestinger new combinations of your own. After you complete your list, try using your new words in a story.

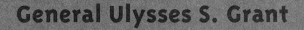

General Ulysses S. Grant

THE GREAT MILITARY HERO of the Union in the Civil War was Ulysses S. Grant (1822–1886). Like Mark Twain, Grant rose from humble beginnings. He was an obscure colonel of a volunteer regiment when the war began. By the time it ended, Abraham Lincoln had made Grant the supreme commander of the Union Army. After Grant accepted Confederate commander Robert E. Lee's surrender, Congress promoted him to full general—a rank that no one but George Washington had held before him. In 1868—the year after Mark Twain met him—Grant was nominated for the presidency by the Republican Party. After Grant had served two terms as president, the two men met again and became close friends.

☞ **Sam meets General Grant.**

Nevada. It was Stewart who introduced Sam to General Ulysses S. Grant.

Sam's arrangement with Senator Stewart did not last long, but he spent enough time in Washington to get a good idea of how the government worked. He was not favorably impressed. Ever afterward, he looked for opportunities to make fun of the government—especially members of Congress.

In December 1867, something even more important happened to Sam. At a reunion gathering of the *Quaker City* passengers in New York City, he met the woman who was to become his wife. Olivia Langdon, or Livy, as she was known, was the sister of Charles Langdon, a young man who had been one of Sam's pals on the *Quaker City*. A great admirer of Sam, Charley was thrilled to have the chance to introduce him to his family. A few nights later, Sam accompanied Livy and her family to a public reading given by the famous English novelist Charles Dickens, who was then on his last tour of America. The author of such classic novels as *Oliver Twist*, *David Copperfield*, and *A Tale of Two Cities*, Dickens was immensely popular in the United States.

Sam was becoming a popular writer himself. In late January he paid his first visit to Hartford, Connecticut, where he talked with Elisha Bliss about writing a book about the *Quaker City* excursion. Although Sam had published a small book the year before, he thought of himself more as a journalist than an "author," and he wasn't sure that writing a big book was something he wanted to do. Bliss was an officer in the American Publishing Company, which specialized in subscription books. Subscription books weren't sold in regular stores, but by agents across the country who went from house to house to sign up buyers before the books were even published.

Subscription-book publishing was very different from regular book publishing. People who bought subscription books generally owned only a few books, and they wanted their books to be big and fat, with lots of pictures. After the Civil War, subscription publishing became a big business, partly because thousands of war veterans were desperate for jobs and were willing to work for salesmen's commissions instead of salaries. This was a new development in book publishing, and it had an important impact on Sam's writing career. Most of his books would be published for the subscription market, and that meant that he would often tailor them to meet the market's special demands for fat books with lots of pictures.

Although Sam was slow to sign a contract with the American Publishing Company, he agreed to write the book and soon set to work on it. He initially figured that he had only to pull his *Quaker City* letters together and make a few changes here and there, but he ended up doing much more new writing than he had expected. The final product was exactly what the subscription market wanted: a big, fat book.

Return to California

BEFORE SAM FINISHED writing *The Innocents Abroad*, he learned that San Francisco's *Alta California* was planning to use his travel letters in a book of its own. Sam didn't think that was fair, so he went back to San Francisco to talk the paper's editors out of their plan. Afterward, he stayed in San Francisco to finish writing his book, and he enlisted a friend, Bret Harte, to help him.

While Sam was in California, he made some money with another little lecture tour, this time talking about the Holy Land. The tour took him back to Nevada, for what would be the last time. At the end of June he pronounced his book finished, and he headed back to the East Coast. He would never see California or Nevada again.

Courting Livy

SAM DELIVERED HIS MANUSCRIPT to Bliss in Hartford, then took a train to Elmira, New York, to visit the Langdon family. He pretended that he was going there to see Charley, but he really wanted to see Livy. He had decided that he wanted to marry her and needed time to get her to accept his proposal.

The Langdons were one of the wealthiest and most important families in Elmira, a growing railroad center near the New York–Pennsylvania border. Livy's father, Jervis Langdon, had made his fortune in the coal business that had grown along with the railroads. As an upper-class Eastern family, the

Bret Harte

ANOTHER 19TH-CENTURY WRITER whose name is closely associated with that of Mark Twain is Bret Harte (1836–1902), who was famous for such short stories as "The Luck of Roaring Camp" and "The Outcasts of Poker Flat." Harte's national reputation as a first-rate writer of Western tales developed just as Sam started to win a reputation of his own. The two men became friends while both were living in San Francisco during the 1860s. Harte edited a literary magazine there, in which he published some of Sam's writings, and he helped Sam edit his manuscript of *The Innocents Abroad*. Sam later turned against Harte for personal reasons (which included Harte's insulting Sam's wife), but their names were forever linked by the establishment of Twain-Harte, a town located in the Sierra Nevada foothills of California.

Langdons could hardly have been more different than the Missouri Clemenses. Not only were they rich, they had very different political and social views. Livy's parents had even been abolitionists at the same time that Sam's relatives had owned slaves.

The Langdons liked Sam. Charley almost worshipped him. However, they were cautious

☞ **Cameo portrait of Livy before Sam met her.**

about allowing Livy to marry. She was 10 years younger than Sam and had long suffered from such poor health that she was considered fragile. In addition, Sam had nothing but his personality and new reputation as a writer to recommend him. His own family counted for little, and his careless dress and strange Southern drawl did not inspire confidence.

After spending a week with the Langdons, Sam wasn't satisfied with the progress he was making with Livy but figured he should leave so he wouldn't wear out his welcome. When it came time to go, he climbed into the back seat of a wagon with Charley, who was accompanying him to the train station, and said his good-byes to the family. The wagon seat wasn't locked down properly. When the wagon lurched forward, the seat flipped over backward, dumping Charley and Sam on the ground. Sam wasn't really hurt, but he saw this as a chance to prolong his visit. He was carried back into the house, and, careful not to "recover" too quickly, he was rewarded with two more weeks of Livy's company.

Toward the end of 1868 Sam began his first really long lecture tour. He visited more than 40 towns spread between Iowa and New York, delivering his "American Vandal Abroad" lecture. It didn't take him long to grow tired of lecturing. He hated the constant travel, the discomfort of sleeping in a different hotel each night, and the dreary sameness of the towns he visited.

Sam wrote to Livy every day while he was on the road and took several breaks from his tour to visit her in Elmira. During one visit, he finally persuaded her marry him. However, he still had to get her parents' approval. Respectable Eastern families were more cautious in those days. While the Langdons liked Sam, they didn't know much about his background. Jervis Langdon asked Sam for the names of people in the West to whom he could write for personal references. Sam gave him six names.

Sam's own account of what happened next can't be proven, but it makes another good story in Mark Twain's legend. After Livy's father got letters from the men to whom he had written for references, he called Sam into his office and read the letters aloud to him. They were a disaster. Their writers not only disapproved of Sam but said he was an awful person. One minister even predicted that Sam would die a drunkard.

When Mr. Langdon finished reading the letters, there was an embarrassing silence. Finally, he said, "What kind of people are these? Haven't you a friend in the world?" Sam meekly replied, "Apparently not." Then Mr. Langdon said, "I'll be your friend, myself. Take the girl. I know you better than they do." Sam and Livy then became officially engaged.

They set their wedding date for almost exactly one year later. Then Sam got back on a train to continue his lecture tour.

Sam finished his tour and turned his attention to correcting the printed proofs of *The Innocents Abroad*. Livy helped him with this tedious work while he stayed with her family in Elmira. The book was published in July. Sam still didn't think of himself an "author." He saw himself as primarily a writer of newspaper articles and humorous sketches. The two books he had published seemed more like accidents than planned efforts.

Settling Down

Now that Sam was about to get married, he needed to settle down. He decided that the best thing he could do would be to buy into a newspaper and make a career of journalism. He borrowed money from Jervis Langdon to buy a one-third interest in the *Buffalo Express* newspaper in upstate New York. He then rented a room in Buffalo and settled into his new role as a newspaper owner and editor.

While Sam was beginning his new life, *The Innocents Abroad* was becoming a fabulous success. It would eventually sell more copies than any other travel book ever published in the United States. Modern authors promote their books by going on what is called the "talk-show circuit," giving interviews on radio and television that are seen and heard by millions of people. In the 19th century, the best way for authors to promote their books was to go on the lecture circuit. In November, Sam began yet another tour in November, lecturing in 60 towns between Rhode Island and Washington, D.C., in less than three months.

On the evening of February 2, 1870, Sam and Livy were married in the parlor of the Langdons' Elmira home. The next day they took a train to Buffalo, accompanied by relatives and a few friends. Sam's lecture tour had kept him too busy to find a new home for himself and Livy, so he had asked a business associate of Mr. Langdon's named Slee, who worked in Buffalo, to find him rooms in a boardinghouse. Concerned about money, he instructed Slee to find rooms that were not expensive.

The wedding party's train arrived in Buffalo, and Slee was waiting at the station with several sleighs ready to take everyone to the place where he had rented rooms for the newlyweds. Sam's and Livy's sleigh became separated from the others, and their journey took so long that Sam wondered if the house to which they were supposed to be headed really existed. When they finally stopped in front of a grand house on Buffalo's fashionable Delaware Avenue, Sam was ready to explode: Slee

☞ **This illustration of Mark Twain, used to advertise** *The Innocents Abroad*, **shows him dressed as an "American vandal."**

Sam and Livy's Buffalo home.

had gotten rooms that were obviously too expensive! But a big surprise awaited him.

The rest of the wedding party had arrived earlier, and a cheery celebration was already going on. Livy then told Sam that they weren't renting rooms in the house; they *owned* the house and everything in it! A wedding gift from her parents, the house had been furnished, staffed with servants, and prepared for the couple's arrival well before the wedding. Everyone but Sam had been in on the secret.

Now just over 34 years old, Sam was a successful author, a part owner of a newspaper, a husband, and the owner of a fine home. He found married life delightfully agreeable, an opinion that would never change. He enjoyed writing for the *Buffalo Express*, and he soon took on the new responsibility of writing a monthly column for a New York magazine called *Galaxy*. His *Galaxy* column paid well and the magazine's owners gave him the freedom to write about almost anything he wanted. Many of his best sketches appeared there.

Around this time, Elisha Bliss talked Sam into writing another book. With a little coaxing, Sam agreed to write about his Western experiences. To Easterners, the West was still a wild and remote region, and the gold and silver discoveries of recent decades there added to its interest. The book Sam would write was *Roughing It*.

New Responsiblities

BETWEEN ALL HIS writing and editing work and his occasional business trips, Sam was very busy. Then suddenly, he was hit by the full weight of family responsibilities. In the spring, Livy's father fell ill with stomach cancer. Sam went with Livy to Elmira to help nurse him and spent many long nights at his father-in-law's bedside. Jervis Langdon's death in August cast a gloom over Sam and Livy's first year of married life. Livy's brother, Charley, took over the family business, and Livy herself received a large inheritance. But, the strain of her father's bout with cancer left Livy exhausted. To make things even more difficult, she was due to have her first baby at the end of the year.

In late August, Emma Nye, an old friend of Livy's, was passing through Buffalo on her way to a teaching job in Detroit. She decided to stay with the Clemenses for a while to help look after Livy and cheer her up. Sadly, she contracted such a bad case of typhoid fever that Livy ended up nursing her. After a month-long illness, Emma died, leaving Livy in an even worse state than she had been before. Finally, in early November, Livy delivered a son, whom she and Sam named Langdon, after her family.

Langdon was born prematurely and was never strong. A few months after he was born, Livy contracted the same fever that had killed her friend Emma. As these medical disasters piled up, it must have seemed to Sam that he was living out one of his boyhood nightmares. For several months he wasn't sure if either Livy or Langdon would survive. It was a terrible time for him, and his worries made it nearly impossible for him to concentrate on writing.

By March 1871 Sam and Livy had experienced so much unhappiness in Buffalo that they decided to move away. Sam put their house and his interest in the newspaper up for sale and took his family back to Elmira, where Livy could recuperate in her sister's home.

Livy's adopted sister, Susan, and her husband, Theodore Crane, lived on a small farm outside Elmira that Jervis Langdon had purchased in 1869 for use as a summer home. When Jervis died, he left the farm to Susan, who lived on it for the rest of her life. Nicknamed "Quarry Farm" after an old stone quarry on the property, the farm had a large, comfortable house with a beautiful view of the Chemung Valley in which Elmira stood.

The farm's quiet and peaceful location seemed to have a restorative effect on visitors, and Sam and Livy would make it their regular summer home over the next 20 years—much like the Quarles family farm had been the Clemens family's home-away-from-home during Sam's youth. All three of Sam's daughters would be born at Quarry Farm, and he would

eventually do much of his most important writing there. His sister-in-law even had a special study built for him, away from the noises of the house.

Through these tumultuous times, Sam kept working on his new book about the West. He also traveled quite a bit, both for business reasons relating to his writing and to sell his interest in the *Buffalo Express*. He decided to move to Hartford, Connecticut, where the American Publishing Company was based. By the end of the summer, he had finished writing *Roughing It*. Afterward, he rented a house in Hartford, to which he moved his family. Hartford would remain his home for the next 20 years, during which time he would transform himself from a Southerner to a New Englander and become a Connecticut "Yankee."

☛ **Sam wrote most of his most famous books in his octogonal Quarry Farm study.**

5
Connecticut Yankee

The Clemens family's move to Connecticut began another phase in Sam's life. Gone were the carefree days of his bachelorhood and uncertainty about his future. He was now a settled family man, one who took his responsibilities seriously. He also finally understood that his true vocation lay in writing books. Moreover, he was becoming famous. *The Innocents Abroad* was a runaway bestseller, and

Roughing It was about to do almost as well. Sam afterward expected every book he wrote to be equally successful.

Sam had first visited Hartford, Connecticut, in 1869 and liked it immensely. Connecticut's capital was a beautiful, prosperous, and genteel New England city that offered a tranquility that both Sam and Livy craved after their unhappy experience in Buffalo. Hartford was also the location of the American Publishing Company, the center of the insurance industry, and the home of the giant Colt Arms Factory. Moreover, Hartford was located midway between Boston and New York City—two cities that Sam would need to visit regularly.

The Clemenses settled in a West Hartford community known as Nook Farm, where they rented a house from Isabella Beecher Hooker, the sister of the Reverend Henry Ward Beecher and Harriet Beecher Stowe. Stowe herself was also a resident of Nook Farm, as were other literary figures. That was another thing that Sam liked about Nook Farm.

Another important resident of the community was the Congregationalist minister Joe Twichell, whom Sam had met earlier and immediately liked. Although Joe and Sam had different views on religion, they always enjoyed each other's company and would remain intimate friends throughout the rest of their lives. Joe helped officiate at Sam and Livy's wedding and he would later preside over other important Clemens family occasions.

Sam hadn't been in Hartford long before he set off on another long lecture tour, which took him back and forth between New England and

Harriet Beecher Stowe

MARK TWAIN'S HARTFORD NEIGHBOR Harriet Beecher Stowe (1811–1896) was the author of *Uncle Tom's Cabin,* a novel that had raised American awareness of the evils of slavery before the Civil War. Published in 1852, the book was the best-selling American novel of the entire 19th century, and some people—including President Abraham Lincoln—credited it with helping to start the war by angering Northerners. Her novel's title character also gave African Americans the expression "Uncle Tom," which they have since applied to black men who behave subserviently around white people. Stowe's novel and Mark Twain's *Adventures of Huckleberry Finn* are now often compared as great antislavery novels.

the Midwest. In March 1872, not long after he concluded the tour, the first of his three daughters, Susy, was born at Quarry Farm. Unfortunately, the joy brought by her birth was soon tempered by grief. Sam and Livy's son, Langdon, died three months later after contracting the bacterial disease diphtheria. Sam would never have another son.

First Trip to England

THAT FALL, Sam made a trip that he had been planning for a long time: his first visit to England. His chief reason for going was to protect the publishing rights to his books in Great Britain. Since international copyright laws didn't exist then, any British publisher could put out a book by an American author without paying royalties or even asking permission. (Some American publishers did the same thing with books by British authors.) Publishers who did that were not breaking any laws, but many people regarded the practice as unethical and called such publishers "pirates."

Throughout his career, Sam lost a lot of money because of pirate publishers in Britain and Canada, and he constantly fought them. When he was in England, he made arrangements for an authorized publisher of *The Innocents Abroad*, and he secured a British

☛ Joe Twichell.

copyright for *Roughing It*. In future years he would have good relations with his British publishers.

A second reason Sam went to England was to arrange for a lecture tour to be conducted on a future visit. He figured that the British would have some interest in him, but he was totally unprepared for the overwhelmingly warm welcome he received when he landed in England. He was treated like visiting royalty and entertained grandly everywhere he went. It was his first taste of celebrity in a foreign country. He had planned to collect notes for a

> "Always do right. This will gratify some people and astonish the rest."
>
> —MARK TWAIN

humorous travel book on the country, but he soon abandoned that idea and concentrated instead on meeting people and sightseeing. When he got home in November, he couldn't wait to return to England, this time with his family, for a longer visit.

The following year, 1873, was an especially important one for Sam. He and Livy decided to settle permanently in Hartford. They bought a large parcel of land in Nook Farm, next to Harriet Beecher Stowe's home, on which to build their own house. That same year they visited England together. Before they went, Sam wrote his first novel.

Mark Twain's First Novel

UNTIL THIS TIME, Sam had never written anything quite like a novel. His big travel books were filled with fiction, but they certainly weren't novels. He had written hundreds of short pieces, but few of them can even be properly described as short stories. Novel writing was thus something that Sam got into almost by accident.

One evening, Sam and Livy were having dinner with two neighbors, Elisabeth and Charles Dudley Warner, and the group got to talking about current fiction. The men made fun of the novels their wives were discussing, and the women challenged them to write something better themselves. Charles was also a professional writer, but, like Sam, he had never written a novel before. Nevertheless, he and Sam accepted their wives' challenge by writing a novel together.

Unlike most of the fiction that Sam had written before, a novel required a long and sensible story line, or plot. It also required fully developed characters—people that readers could become interested in and care about. To create these features, Sam drew on characters and a plot with which he was already familiar. He started his portion of the book he was writing with Charles Dudley Warner with 11 chapters about a family moving from eastern Tennessee to Missouri. The story was nothing less than a retelling of his own family's history. He then turned the manuscript over to Warner, who continued the story by adding new characters and plot twists of his own. For several months the two neighbors alternated writing new chapters and tinkering with each other's work until the book was finished.

The resulting novel was *The Gilded Age*. A complicated saga of two loosely connected families, it is often confusing and difficult to follow. Its story deals with the development of the Western frontier, dreams of getting rich, political corruption, women's education, coal mining, and murder.

The book's central theme was one close to Sam's heart: the disastrous consequences of a family's pinning its hopes on the acquisition of easy riches. In the book, the Hawkins family counts on getting rich by selling a huge tract of land in eastern Tennessee. That dream nearly ruins the Hawkinses, just as a similar dream about Tennessee land had once nearly ruined the Clemens family.

The Gilded Age also contains one of Sam's finest characters: Colonel Beriah (or Mulberry) Sellers. Inspired by one of Jane Lampton Clemens's relatives, Sellers is always full of grand schemes to get rich. His motto is "There's millions in it!" While most of his schemes come to nothing, he remains loveable, and he is the focus of most of the humor in *The Gilded Age*.

Colonel Sellers was such a great character that a San Francisco man wrote a play about him, and cast the popular actor John T. Raymond in the lead role. Since the Sellers character was stolen from *The Gilded Age*, Sam managed to get control of the play himself. The play toured the United States for 10 years and made Sam even more money than the novel did.

In addition to raising Sam's income, the play's success encouraged him to try play-

Colonel Sellers blowing bubbly dreams of wealth.

writing himself, but that was something he was never very good at. However, he did publish a sequel to *The Gilded Age* in 1892: *The American Claimant*. That book is built around Colonel Sellers's claim that he is the rightful heir to an English earldom—another idea inspired by Sam's relative.

Travel and Family

A MONTH AFTER FINISHING *The Gilded Age* with Warner, Sam again sailed to England, this time with Livy and 14-month-old Susy. Like his previous trip, this visit was a triumph. Sam gave a few lectures, but he saved the bulk of that work for yet another trip on his own. Less than a week after returning to New York with his family, he embarked on his third trip to England, this time to make a three-month lecture tour.

Sam loved almost everything about England. In a letter to a friend after his first visit, he had written that "Rural England is too absolutely beautiful to be left out doors—ought to be under a glass case." He had always enjoyed reading about history, and his visits to England moved him to read quite a bit about English history. This would later inspire him to write two of his most famous novels—but first he had other writing to do.

The Adventures of Tom Sawyer

IN JUNE 1874 Sam and Livy's second daughter, Clara, was born. That same summer, Sam worked on the first novel he could call entirely his own: *The Adventures of Tom Sawyer*. This book draws heavily on Sam's own boyhood. It is set in a place much like the Hannibal of Sam's youth, and many of its characters were modeled on Sam's relatives and friends. For several years, Sam had been thinking a lot about his boyhood. Many details and incidents in *The Adventures of Tom Sawyer* came straight out of his memories. In his preface to the book, he said that the "odd superstitions touched upon were all prevalent among children and slaves in the West at the period of this story." He also said that part of his purpose in writing the book was "to try to pleasantly remind adults of what they once were themselves, and of how they felt and thought and talked, and what queer enterprises they sometimes engaged in."

Sam continued to work on *The Adventures of Tom Sawyer* through 1875. Meanwhile, his family moved into their house before it was completely finished. Built on five acres above a picturesque stream, the family's new home was three stories high, and had 19 rooms and five balconies. Its steeply gabled roofs, colorful bricks, and unusual decorative features gave it a striking appearance that reflected the uniqueness of its most famous resident. The Clemenses entertained guests in their new home almost constantly. A large number of leading literary figures, artists, and political leaders visited them there.

Through the rest of the 1870s Sam remained quietly busy with various writing projects, occasional speeches, and family matters. He also tried his hand at inventing, and he took out several government patents (documents that protected his inventions). His only successful invention, however, was a self-pasting scrapbook, which, for a while, brought in as much money as his written books.

Sam finished writing *The Adventures of Tom Sawyer* in the middle of 1875, but the

Collect Odd Superstitions

Part of Mark Twain's goal in writing *The Adventures of Tom Sawyer* was to remind adults of what it was like to be children and to recall the "odd superstitions" in which children sometimes believe. Superstitions are ideas that people believe are true even though they cannot be proven and may even go against nature. For example, Tom and his friends believe that:

- Dead cats can be used to cure warts.
- Lost marbles can be found with magical incantations, but witchcraft sometimes makes the incantations fail.
- Oaths signed in blood with and accompanied by special incantations cannot be broken.
- Bread loaves that contain quicksilver (mercury) will float over drowned bodies.
- Pirate treasure can be found under the shadows of dead tree limbs at midnight.

Nowadays, we laugh at such superstitions. But, many people still believe in others, such as crossing their fingers for luck or avoiding the number 13.

WHAT YOU NEED
- Pen or pencil
- Notepad or sheets of paper

Make a list of all the superstitions that you, your friends, and members of your family can think of, then ask your friends whether they believe in them. Write a Y for each yes and an N for each no. When you are done, count the Ys and Ns to determine which superstitions most people believe.

These examples will get you started. Add as many more you can.

- When a groundhog sees its shadow on February 2, there will be six more weeks of winter.
- Four-leaf clovers bring good luck.
- Friday the 13th is an unlucky day.
- Lightning never strikes the same place twice.
- Knocking on wood protects you against bad luck.
- Saying "bless you" after a person sneezes wards off evil spirits.

The Restless Traveler

IN THE SPRING of 1877, Sam went to Bermuda with Joe Twichell for a short vacation. The island's beauty and leisurely atmosphere provided the men a pleasant change of pace. Both friends wanted to return there again soon, but it would be 30 years before they would go back.

By 1878 Sam was becoming restless again, and Elisha Bliss was after him to write another book. Sam decided to take his family to Europe, where he would gather material for a new travel book. He signed a book contract, and in April the family sailed from New York to Germany. Everyone prepared for the trip by studying German. They even took a German-speaking governess with them to help tend the children. During the year and a half that they were gone, they spent most of their time in Germany and Switzerland, but they also visited Italy, France, Belgium, the Netherlands, and Great Britain.

While he was in Europe, Sam struggled to write the book that would become *A Tramp Abroad*. His other travel books had grown naturally out of travels he had undertaken for reasons other than writing a book. Sam found that writing a book at the same time he was *doing* the traveling was more difficult than he had expected. Having his whole family with

book didn't come out until the end of the following year. It did not have the same huge success that his travel books had enjoyed, but it sold well and would continue to sell well long after Sam died. *The Adventures of Tom Sawyer* is one of the rare books that has never gone out of print. In the 130 years since it was first published, it has been translated into almost every major language in the world and enjoyed by untold millions of people.

Sam in 1880.

him didn't make his task any easier. Although he had his wife and a governess to look after his young daughters, he liked to spend time with them himself. In addition, he was often distracted by the complications of finding suitable lodgings for five people, moving bulky luggage from place to place, and socializing with people whom his family met.

What finally saved Sam's book was a visit by Joe Twichell, who caught up with the

Keep a Scrapbook

Mark Twain's only successful invention was his self-pasting scrapbook. Over the years, he had kept several scrapbooks, but he'd grown tired of pasting articles and pictures into them with glue—which, at the time, was much messier to use than the products we have today. Around 1872 he hit on a clever idea: scrapbook pages with strips of glue already on them, so that all one had to do was wet the glue with water and press pictures down on the pages. After he patented the idea, a company sold "Mark Twain's Patent Self-Pasting Scrap Books" in many sizes and models. His scrapbooks haven't been made for a long time, but they can occasionally be found in antique stores and on eBay. For this activity, you'll find it easier to buy a modern scrapbook with self-adhesive pages covered with clear sheets of celluloid, which can be found in most stationery stores and drugstores.

Scrapbooks are fun because they can be used to collect almost anything that can be pressed flat within a book. Scrapbooks are often built around themes, such as family pictures, animals, cars, movies, stories in the news, or anything else of interest. Choose a theme, then look for related stories and pictures in newspapers and magazines. Get permission to cut them out, and put them in the scrapbook. Label each entry with its date and source. Be sure to keep your scrapbooks, as they will give you great pleasure when you are older.

Ideas for scrapbook themes

- Mark Twain and other favorite authors

- Stories about traveling to Mars (which may happen in your lifetime!)
- Endangered animal species
- Censorship in schools
- Modern inventions

WHAT YOU NEED
- ✳ Pictures, newspapers, magazines, and other items
- ✳ Scrapbook with self-adhesive pages
- ✳ Scissors

Clemenses at Baden-Baden, Germany, in August. Sam and Joe then spent a month sightseeing together in Germany and the Swiss Alps. Having Joe travel with him gave Sam a valuable idea that he used in *A Tramp Abroad*: that of an invented travel companion, whom he named Harris. The book begins with its narrator (who is never named) announcing that his book is about a walking tour that he made through Europe. However, while the narrator always *talks* about walking through Europe, he actually almost never walks anywhere. Instead, he always finds excuses for getting from place to place on trains, carriages, animals, boats, and even a raft.

Throughout his wanderings, the narrator talks freely about the places he visits and the unusual sights that he sees. He travels with a man named Harris, who contributes a lot of the book's humor by constantly criticizing and complaining. The relationship between the book's narrator and Harris is much like that of a modern comedy team made up of a straight man and a comic. While the straight man tries to act serious, the comic cracks jokes and says disrespectful things that the straight man would never say.

☛ **Struggling to write *A Tramp Abroad*.**

Sam enjoyed his European trip, but he was relieved to get home and finish writing his book. He was especially anxious to get back to American food.

The Prince and The Pauper

IN JUNE 1880, three months after *A Tramp Abroad* was published, Sam and Livy's third daughter, Jean, was born. Sam was already working on a new novel that was both a labor of love and something quite different from anything that he had written before: *The Prince and the Pauper*. Inspired by his fascination with English history, he set this story in 16th-century England, in the year King Henry VIII died.

The prince of the book's title is Edward VI. This character is named after the real son of King Henry who became king himself upon his father's death in 1547. The pauper, a character that Sam created from his imagination, is a boy named Tom Canty, who lives a life of terrible poverty and who dreams about being a prince.

One day, when Tom is sent out to beg, he wanders all the way to the royal palace. Prince Edward happens to see a guard mistreat Tom, and he invites Tom inside the palace, where

Bake Missouri-Fried Corn Pone

Sam grew very tired of European foods while he was traveling, and he often found himself longing for his favorite American dishes. One of those was corn pone, a type of flat cake made from cornmeal dough. Invented by Native Americans long before Europeans settled in North America, corn pone is also called "ashcake," "johnnycake," and "battercake." This recipe makes about one dozen pones.

WHAT YOU NEED
Adult supervision required
* Medium-sized mixing bowl
* 1 egg
* 2 tablespoons sugar
* 1 tablespoon baking powder
* 1 teaspoon baking soda
* 1 teaspoon salt
* 3 to 4 tablespoons vegetable oil
* Medium-sized skillet
* 1¾ cups buttermilk
* 2 cups cornmeal
* Spatula
* Cooling rack

In the mixing bowl, combine the egg, sugar, baking powder, baking soda, and salt and beat well into a batter. Place 1 tablespoon oil in the skillet and heat over medium heat.

As the skillet is heating, stir the buttermilk and cornmeal into the batter until it reaches an even consistency.

When the oil is hot, pour ¼ cup batter into the skillet for each cake, or pone. Turn the pones over with a spatula as they brown on the bottom, just as you would cook a pancake. When the pones are brown on both sides, transfer them to a cooling rack.

Repeat the cooking process, adding oil to the skillet as needed, until the batter has been used. Serve while still warm.

he feeds him and asks him about his life. Tom tells the prince about some of the games he plays:

→ *We dance and sing about the Maypole in Cheapside; we play in the sand, each covering his neighbor up; and times we make mud pastry—oh, the lovely mud, it hath not its like for delightfulness in all the world!—we do fairly wallow in the mud, sir, saving your worship's presence.* ←

The prince, who is usually shut up in the palace, replies,

→ *Oh, prithee, say no more, 'tis glorious! If that I could but clothe me in raiment like to thine, and strip my feet, and revel in the mud once, just once, with none to rebuke me or forbid, meseemeth I could forego the crown.* ←

Envious of Tom's freedom and of the games he plays with his pauper friends, Prince Edward suggests switching clothes, just for fun. Afterward, the boys stand before a mirror together and discover that they look almost exactly alike. Then, through a series of accidents, the real prince is mistaken for Tom and is roughly tossed out of the palace.

After the boys are separated, each of them tries telling everyone he meets who he really is, but no one believes either of them. Tom is scared that when the ailing king finds out who he is, he will be executed. However, even King Henry thinks that Tom is his own son, and orders the boy not to say otherwise. Tom becomes stuck in the palace, and he is proclaimed king after King Henry dies. Meanwhile, the real Edward goes through many exciting adventures in his quest to find someone who will believe his story so that he can claim his rightful throne.

Sam so loved writing this book that he almost hoped he would never finish it. He especially enjoyed playing with 16th-century

☞ **The prince entertains Tom Canty in the palace.**

English language. His biggest fan was his daughter Susy, who thought that the book's courtly language was especially wonderful. Later, when his daughters were a little older, they and their friends enjoyed putting on little dramatic productions of *The Prince and the Pauper*. Sometimes Sam himself joined in by playing the adult hero, Miles Hendon.

Although *The Prince and the Pauper* is, on the whole, very different from Sam's other books, there are similarities. For example, the pauper boy, Tom Canty, is a lot like Tom Sawyer, and the games that he plays beside London's River Thames are much like the games that Tom Sawyer plays beside the Mississippi River. The book also deals with themes that Sam explored in other books: the confusion of identities and people who make claims they cannot prove.

Returning to the Mississippi River

SAM'S NEXT BOOK was *Life on the Mississippi*. Years earlier, he had recalled his steamboat piloting days in a series of magazine articles. What he wanted to do now was write a book about the river that would be recognized as an authoritative work—the type of book to which anyone who wants information on the Mississippi River would refer. He planned to use his articles in his new book, but he also needed to gather fresh information. To do that, he had to go back to the river.

The following spring, Sam and two companions took a train to St. Louis, where they boarded the steamboat *Gold Dust* for a leisurely voyage down the Mississippi to New Orleans. It was the first time in over 20 years that Sam had been on the great river. One of the pilots knew him, and he allowed Sam to take occasional turns at the helm. Steering a steamboat down the Mississippi brought back many pleasant memories, and Sam wondered if he had made a mistake by leaving the river.

Much had changed on the Mississippi River since the Civil War, and Sam didn't like all the changes. For example, the U.S. Army Corps of Engineers had cleared many parts of the river and added markers, including electric lights, to make it safer for boats. These changes were good, but they destroyed some of the romance of piloting. An even greater change had resulted from the huge expansion of railroads, which had taken away most of the river's passenger traffic and commerce. The number of boats on the river had greatly decreased. Even worse, the power and independence of the pilots had been so reduced that they now had to take orders from their captains!

"My own luck has been curious all my literary life; I never could tell a lie that anybody would doubt, nor a truth that anybody would believe."

—MARK TWAIN

Hannibal contain some of Sam's most moving memories of his boyhood.

Writing *Life on the Mississippi* kept Sam busy through the rest of the year. He then turned his attention to a novel that he had started more than five years earlier, but had repeatedly set aside. This was the book that has come to be recognized as not only Mark Twain's greatest work, but one of the greatest American novels ever written: *Adventures of Huckleberry Finn*.

Adventures of Huckleberry Finn

SAM HAD STARTED THIS NOVEL as a simple sequel to *The Adventures of Tom Sawyer*. Indeed, *Adventures of Huckleberry Finn* picks up exactly where *The Adventures of Tom Sawyer* leaves off, with Huck agreeing to live with the Widow Douglas in order to become respectable enough to join Tom Sawyer's robber gang. The opening chapters of the book are similar to those of *The Adventures of Tom Sawyer*, but the book soon takes a turn in a very different direction. Like *The Adventures of Tom Sawyer*, *Adventures of Huckleberry Finn* is a fine adventure story that is filled with humor. However, it also deals with

 Horace Bixby's *City of Baton Rouge.*

On his return trip from New Orleans, Sam rode on the *City of Baton Rouge*, a steamboat captained by his old teacher, Horace Bixby. Bixby had become one of the true legends of steamboating, and it was fitting that he was now a captain. After Sam and his companions reached St. Louis, Sam continued up the river on his own all the way to St. Paul, Minnesota. Along the way, he spent several days in Hannibal, revisiting old haunts and seeing old friends. *Life on the Mississippi*'s chapters on something much more important: human equality and dignity.

The novel does a wonderful job of exposing the evils of slavery and makes pointed fun of white people's pretensions of being superior to black people. Sam modeled the novel's central black character, Jim, on the slave Uncle Daniel, whom he had known when he was a boy. Like Uncle Daniel, Jim is honest, intelligent, and warmhearted. In a story populated by ignorant, greedy, dishonest, and morally corrupt white people, Jim emerges as the novel's most truly noble character. Along the way, he teaches Huck about true human dignity.

The novel's central story line follows the teenage Huck running away from St. Petersburg, Missouri, to escape from his abusive and alcoholic father. Huck's flight becomes more complicated when he joins up with Jim, a slave who is also fleeing from St. Petersburg. Jim fears that his owner will sell him "down the river," where he will face the horrors of plantation slavery and be far away from his wife and children. Jim wants to make his way into free territory and earn enough money either to buy his wife and children's freedom or to pay abolitionists to steal them out of slavery.

After Huck and Jim find a large raft, they plan to float down the Mississippi to the Ohio River. There they hope to sell the raft and buy steamboat passage up the Ohio into free terri-

tory. Unfortunately, they drift by the Ohio River during a foggy night and continue going south. Along the way, they have many adventures and meet many colorful characters, including nasty con artists who claim to be a duke and king and take control of the raft.

As the story begins, Huck does not even regard Jim as fully human. Huck himself is a boy who was once considered a social outcast among white people. Before the Widow Douglas took him into her home, he was the homeless son of a worthless town drunk. He loafed around the town, didn't go to school, and was generally despised by the parents of other children his age. Nevertheless, Huck has grown up trained by the customs of white society to think of himself as superior to African Americans simply because he is white. An example of his prejudice comes out one night on the raft, when he happens to overhear Jim crying about his children, whom he may never see again. Huck thinks to himself, "I do believe he cared just as much for his people as white folks does for their'n. It don't seem natural, but I reckon it's so." By the end of the novel, Huck realizes that Jim is not only fully human, but also an exceptionally fine friend— one for whom he is willing to sacrifice his own soul. He thinks that because he has helped Jim escape from slavery he will go to hell instead of to heaven.

Be a Movie Critic

Novels and movies are very different forms of art. It's probably impossible to turn a novel into a movie in a way that will please everyone. To keep movies that are adapted from novels within reasonable lengths, scenes from the novels are left out, characters are combined or dropped, and details that are thoroughly explained in the novels may be skipped over. It would be unfair to expect any movie to be completely true to the book on which it is based. However, it *is* fair to expect a movie to do the best job of adapting the novel that it can.

Many movies have been made from Mark Twain's books, especially *The Adventures of Tom Sawyer*, *Adventures of Huckleberry Finn*, *The Prince and the Pauper*, and *A Connecticut Yankee in King Arthur's Court*. This activity will help you understand why watching a movie isn't the same as reading a book.

WHAT YOU NEED

❋ Video cassette or DVD of a movie made from a Mark Twain story

❋ Book on which the movie is based

❋ Pen or pencil

❋ Note paper

❋ Television and appropriate playback device

Rent, buy, or borrow a movie made from one of Mark Twain's stories, such as *Huckleberry Finn*. Before watching it, read the original book carefully, and list the most important events that happen in it. Then think about *meaning* of the story: What is it really about? For example, is it simply about boys having fun? About testing friendship? About overcoming one's fears? Write down the most important ideas you find in the book—the ideas you think should be in a film version.

Watch the movie. Check your notes to see how it compares to the original story. Afterward, write a brief review of the movie, pointing out where it

☛ **Tom and Huck reveal their treasure, in the first film adaptation of *The Adventures of Tom Sawyer*.**

☛ **Scene from the first film adaptation of *Adventures of Huckleberry Finn*.**

succeeds and where it fails in being true to Mark Twain's story. Suggest what could have been done to make the film better.

If you enjoy this exercise, watch another film version of the same story and notice how it differs from the first version. Does it include the same episodes? Does it depict the main characters in the same way? Does it seem to be trying to make different points? The ability to notice such differences is what you'll need to be become a film critic.

Adventures of Huckleberry Finn is a great book because of its depictions of Jim's essential nobility and Huck's growing awareness of the common humanity of all people. Much of the story's power comes from the fact that the entire book is narrated by Huck himself, who does the right thing by helping Jim, even though he thinks he is doing the wrong thing. Having Huck tell the story in his own words makes the book seem more real and natural. In fact, using the character of an ignorant boy to narrate the story was something entirely new in literature. There is nothing artificial or strained about the way that people talk in Adventures of Huckleberry Finn. At the time the book came out, some people called its language coarse and vulgar and said it wasn't fit for children to read. However, the novel changed the course of American literature by helping to free writers from trying to imitate the great "literary" writers of the past.

Sam finished writing Adventures of Huckleberry Finn in the middle of 1883. He then worked on several other writing projects and dabbled with his pet inventions. One was a board game that he patented and sold as "Mark Twain's Memory Builder." He based it on a game he played with his children that helped them remember dates in English history. Unfortunately, Sam's game was far too complicated to ever become popular.

Business Matters

SAM WAS ALWAYS INTERESTED in new inventions and gadgets. In the late 1870s, not long after Alexander Graham Bell invented the telephone, Sam had a phone installed in his own house. His may have been the first private home in the world to have one. He also had an electric burglar alarm installed. The device rang so many false alarms that Sam thought it caused more trouble than burglars and wrote a funny story about it.

Sam and Joe Twichell tried to learn how to ride a bicycle one summer, and that experience made for another funny story. Bicycles were a new invention, and Sam found riding them more difficult than riding a horse—and he never much liked horseback riding, either. The bicycle of 1884 was not like a modern bike. It had a tiny rear wheel and a front wheel as tall as a man; to get onto the seat, riders had to climb up as high as they would climb to get on a horse. In fact, riding one of those early bicycles was a lot like riding a horse, except that the bicycles—unlike horses—almost always fell over when they stopped moving.

At the end of 1884 Sam began his last and longest lecture tour in the United States. For four months he and George Washington Cable, a well-known Southern writer, traveled around the East and delivered more than 100

Take the Needle-and-Thread Test

In *Adventures of Huckleberry Finn*, Huck dresses up as a girl so he can sneak into St. Petersburg to gather news without being recognized. A new villager named Judith Loftus invites him into her home and talks to him for a while but soon guesses that Huck is actually a boy. She secretly puts him to a few tests to learn if she is right. One of her tests is asking Huck to thread a needle for her. Huck holds a piece of thread steady and pushes a needle toward it. Mrs. Loftus afterward tells him that a real girl would do the opposite: hold the needle steady and push the thread toward it.

Do males and females really thread needles differently? Sam must not have been sure himself. When the character Miles Hendon threads a needle in *The Prince and the Pauper*, he does it in a way

Name	M/F	Sewing Experience	Moves Thread	Moves Needle
TOTALS			Moves Thread	Moves Needle
Men				
Women				

exactly opposite to the way that Huck does it in *Adventures of Huckleberry Finn*. You be the judge.

WHAT YOU NEED
Adult supervision recommended

* Needle (preferably one with a large hole and a dull point)
* Piece of thread that will fit the needle's hole
* Lined paper
* Pencil or pen

Draw four columns on a sheet of lined paper: 1 wide column on the left and 5 narrow columns on the right. Label the first column "Name," the second column "Male/Female," the third column "Sewing Experience," the fourth column "Moves Thread," and the fifth column "Moves Needle."

Without explaining what you are trying to learn, take the needle and thread to both male and female friends and relatives, one at a time. (Do not give the needle to young children.) Ask each person to help you by threading the needle. Watch carefully to see whether the person moves the thread or the needle. Record your findings on the paper, indicating the person's gender in the second column and sewing experience ("none," "some," or "a lot") in the third column. Summarize your findings at the bottom of the paper, indicating how many males and females move the thread, and how many move the needle. Do men and women actually thread needles differently? Or did Sam make up the whole idea? Is there a difference between experienced and inexperienced sewers?

lectures in more than a dozen states and parts of Canada. In each performance, both men did readings from their own books. Cable added variety by singing a few songs. Sam's readings included selections from *Adventures of Huckleberry Finn*, which was published at about the time that the lecture tour ended.

The tour was the most exhausting one that Sam had undertaken up to that time, and he renewed his vow to never lecture again. The tour also strained his friendship with Cable, whose habits were very different from his own. By the end of the tour, Sam was almost ready to throttle Cable. He may have been thinking of Cable when he later wrote *Tom Sawyer Abroad*, in which Huck Finn says, "There ain't no surer way to find out whether you like people or hate them than to travel with them."

Mark Twain the Publisher

DURING THE LATE 1880s Sam devoted a great deal of his time to business matters and neglected his writing. His biggest venture was forming his own publishing company. He had never been completely happy with his publishers, and he thought that having his own company would increase the profits of his

Susy, Livy, Clara, and Jean in 1884.

books. He named his new firm Charles L. Webster & Company, after his nephew Charles Webster, whom he put in charge and made a junior partner. Webster was actually Sam's nephew by marriage. He was married to Annie Moffett, the daughter of Sam's sister Pamela.

The new company started out well by making *Adventures of Huckleberry Finn* its first book. Not long afterward, it published

109

Charles L. Webster.

another book that was even more successful: the Civil War memoirs of Ulysses S. Grant. Grant had commanded the Union Army, and he was regarded as a national hero. After the war, he was twice elected president of the United States. After he left office in 1877, however, he fell on hard times. Thanks to a crooked partner, the stock-brokerage business he went into failed, leaving him broke.

In those days, former presidents did not receive pension incomes—a fact that Grant's embarrassing situation would help to change. Sam was a great admirer of General Grant, whom he counted as a personal friend. When he learned that Grant was considering publishing his memoirs to raise money for his family, Sam persuaded him to sign with Charles L. Webster and offered him generous royalty terms.

Grant's health was failing rapidly, and he barely managed to complete his memoirs before dying in mid-1885. Sam's company did a marvelous job of printing and selling the memoirs, which were issued in two handsome volumes. Using the subscription-book technique of selling books door-to-door before they are published, which Sam had learned from the American Publishing Company, the publishing company made *The Personal Memoirs of U. S. Grant* a giant bestseller. Sam was immensely proud when he later paid Grant's widow more than $400,000 in royalties—an astronomical sum in those days.

Charles L. Webster quickly gained recognition as an important publishing company. This would have been a good thing, except for the fact that these early successes gave Sam the foolish idea that everything he touched would turn to gold. That mistake would lead him into making bad business decisions. Even worse, it drew him away from what he should really have been doing—writing books.

A Connecticut Yankee in King Arthur's Court

DESPITE THIS and other distractions, however, Sam did manage to complete one more major novel before the decade was out: *A Connecticut Yankee in King Arthur's Court*. Like *The Prince and the Pauper*, this novel is set in England's past. However, it was a very different kind of book, and Sam didn't intend it for younger readers.

Hank Morgan, the book's "Yankee," is a 19th-century American who is knocked out in a fight. He wakes up in 6th-century England, in the time when Arthur was king.

By the time Hank realizes he isn't dreaming, he is in a dungeon, waiting to be burned at the stake because he is believed to be a monster. However, he happens to know that an eclipse of the sun is due at the moment he is to be executed. He uses that knowledge to make everyone believe that he is so a powerful magician that he can blot out—and bring back—the sun.

King Arthur rewards Hank for restoring the sun by making him his chief minister. Hank then becomes the most powerful person in the kingdom and works to modernize England. In the 19th century, he was the foreman of the Colt Arms Factory in Hartford, so he knows all about modern tools and machinery. Even more important to Hank is his goal to modernize England's political and social system. He wants to abolish slavery and make England a republic, just like the United States.

During Hank's 10 years in England, he accomplishes a great deal. However, age-old customs prove almost impossible to change, and Hank confronts powerful enemies in Merlin the magician and the established Church. Eventually, everything Hank creates collapses, and he returns to his own time after Merlin casts a spell on him that makes him sleep for 13 centuries.

A Connecticut Yankee in King Arthur's Court is a powerful story that gives readers many serious ideas to think about. It is also fun to read as Hank introduces medieval

Plan a Newspaper

In *A Connecticut Yankee in King Arthur's Court*, Hank Morgan says that one of the first things needed in a new country is a newspaper: "You can't resurrect a dead nation without it." He trains reporters and builds printing presses in 6th-century England, and he calls his first newspaper the *Camelot Weekly Hosannah and Literary Volcano*.

Get together with a few friends and plan a newspaper of your own!

WHAT YOU NEED

❋ Paper

❋ Pencil or pen

❋ Computer and printer (optional)

Make a list of the types of stories that your paper will cover. They may be about your school, your church, your family, your neighborhood, or anything you want. Each person should be assigned to write a story on a different kind of subject, such as politics, society, entertainment, sports, or gossip. Anyone who is good at drawing can supply illustrations.

After you get together and compare your stories, choose a name for your paper. (Fictional newspaper names used in Mark Twain's works include *Daily American Earthquake, Daily Battering-Ram, The Daily Warwhoop, The Avalanche, The Morning Howl,* and *The Moral Volcano.*) If you are handy with a computer, put the stories together and see if you can print a page that looks better than this page from the Camelot newspaper that Hank Morgan created.

List the "Little Conveniences"

In *A Connecticut Yankee in King Arthur's Court,* Hank Morgan gets stuck in sixth-century England. He is given fine robes to wear and lives in the castle's best rooms. Nevertheless, he soon starts missing things he was used to in the 19th century. What he most misses aren't "big" modern inventions like telephones and trains, but what he calls the "little conveniences." In the sixth century there are no mirrors, no soap, no matches, no books, no pens, no paper or ink, and not even any glass for windows.

Try to imagine living in Sam Clemens's time. What modern conveniences would you most miss if you were suddenly thrown back to the late 19th century? Airplanes, rocketships, radio and television, cell phones, and computers are the sorts of things that Hank Morgan would call "big" things. They are important, to be sure, but they are mostly things that we can do without. What you should be concerned with here are the modern "little conveniences"—things that even Sam didn't have in the 19th century, such as zippers, ballpoint pens, plastic baggies, paper clips, battery-powered flashlights, and running water.

WHAT YOU NEED

* Pencil or pen
* Note pad or lined paper

Write down the modern little conveniences you depend on most. Look around the rooms of your home, and think about each little thing you rely upon every day. Imagine finding yourself in Sam Clemens's time. What little things do we use most often now that didn't exist then? If you're not sure whether something was available in the 19th century, look it up in an encyclopedia, or ask a parent or teacher about it. Write down the most important little things that didn't exist in the 1800s.

Ask your parents and friends to make their own lists, and compare yours with theirs. This will give you a good idea of how different everyday life was in Mark Twain's time. You'll also be surprised to discover how many of the little things that we now take for granted are modern inventions.

England to such modern inventions as dynamite, rockets, telephones, newspapers, railroads, and steamships. In one scene, Hank smokes a pipe inside the helmet he is wearing. Several knights preparing to attack him instead meekly surrender because they think he is a fire-breathing dragon. In another scene, Hank reluctantly participates in a great tournament. The knights all wear armor, ride great warhorses, and fight with lances and heavy swords. Hank causes a sensation when he rides out on a small horse and is wearing only a cloth gymnast's suit. He fights the knights with a lasso, which he uses to rope and tie them—just like an American cowboy lassoing cattle.

Sam may be considered a true pioneer of science fiction writing. *A Connecticut Yankee in King Arthur's Court* was one of the first time-travel stories ever written. It was published six years before H. G. Wells's *The Time Machine*.

The 1880s were among the most productive, most prosperous, and happiest years of Sam's life. He had a wonderful home and family, he was the most popular author in America, and he was making a great deal of money from his writing and from his publishing company. Unfortunately, these good things were not to last.

6

At Home and Abroad

During the early 1890s three of Sam's greatest interests came together—with disastrous results. He was always fascinated by modern gadgets and inventions—which we can clearly see in *A Connecticut Yankee in King Arthur's Court*. He also had a lifelong interest in finding an easy way to get rich. Even though he probably made more money from writing and lecturing than almost any other author of his time, he wasn't satisfied. Instead of concentrating on doing what he did best, he was always looking for investment opportunities that promised fat returns. It's no

☞ **The Paige typesetting machine.**

surprise that an invention involving something dear to his heart caught his eye: an automatic typesetting machine.

Typesetting had been invented four centuries earlier, when the German inventor Johannes Gutenberg created a printing press that used movable metal type. When Sam worked in printshops, printing had changed very little in 400 years. It remained a slow, tedious job done by hand, one piece of type at a time. The worth of printers was measured by how fast and accurately they could set type. Sam was always open to any idea that would make typesetting faster.

Paige's Typesetting Machine

In 1880 Sam had met James Paige, a Hartford inventor who was working on a machine to set type automatically. A person using the machine had merely to sit down in front of a large keyboard—similar to that of a typewriter—and type each line. The machine put all the pieces of type in place automatically. Sam was captivated by Paige's machine, which he thought a greater invention than the telephone, telegraph, locomotive, cotton gin, or sewing machine.

It wasn't long before Sam began investing in the machine. By 1886 he was Paige's partner, and he was supporting Paige's work at the rate of about $3,000 a month. It was a huge amount of money, but Sam was confident that the machine would eventually repay him many times over. He filled his notebooks with calculations of how much money thousands of the machines would make for him. Not even *The Gilded Age*'s Colonel Sellers could have been more optimistic.

Paige was a true genius, and his machine was indeed a marvel. When it worked properly, it could set type six times faster than the fastest person could do by hand. Unfortunately, it rarely worked properly for very long. As Paige continually tinkered with the machine to perfect it, Sam sank more and more money into it. Meanwhile, his publishing company was starting to lose money, mainly because of the poorly chosen books it was publishing.

Living in Europe

BY 1891 FAMILY FINANCES were looking very bleak. Sam and Livy concluded that they had to do something drastic to cut back on spending. Their grand house, with its large staff of servants, was their biggest expense, so they decided to live in Europe for a year to save money. In June they closed down the house and took a steamship to France.

Over the next several years, Sam and his family moved around France, Germany, Switzerland, and Italy. They stayed for a few weeks or a few months at each of many different places, including several health spas, where Livy hoped to get relief from rheumatism. Sam did some writing, but he was constantly distracted by his business worries. In just three years, he made four trips back to the United States to check on his interests. Things got progressively worse, and his publishing

☛ Henry H. Rogers.

company declared bankruptcy in April 1894. After that disaster, Sam put all his hopes for the future in the Paige typesetting machine.

With the help of his friend Henry H. Rogers, a Standard Oil Company executive, Sam arranged to have Paige's machine tested at a Chicago newspaper plant that already had 32 Mergenthaler Linotype machines working smoothly. Paige's machine set type by moving individual metal pieces, while Mergenthaler's machine poured hot lead into molds a whole line at a time (hence, "line o'type"). During the test, Paige's machine set type faster than the others, but it repeatedly broke down. Newspapers had no time to waste with such an unreliable machine. That was the end of Paige's typesetting machine. Otto Mergenthaler's Linotype machine dominated the typesetting business, and Mergenthaler eventually collected all the riches of which Sam had long dreamed.

The failure of the Paige typesetting machine wiped out every cent of the hundreds of thousands of dollars that Sam had invested in it. It was his worst nightmare come true. He must have felt as though he had inherited his father's knack for business failure. Nevertheless, despite these worries and nearly constant traveling, Sam wrote several of his best short stories, many essays, and several novels during these years. He finished one of these novels, *Pudd'nhead Wilson*, while the family was living near Florence, Italy.

Pudd'nhead Wilson

Pudd'nhead Wilson is a very serious book, but it has its share of humor, as well as a prince-and-pauper theme. It is set in a Missouri town on the Mississippi River that closely resembles Sam's hometown of Hannibal. Its title character, David Wilson, is a young lawyer who comes to the town from the North in 1830. The day he arrives, he makes a peculiar remark that no one can understand. Since he appears to be a fool, he is permanently branded a "puddinghead." For 20 years he never gets a client for a legal case and has to do surveying work to make his living. Meanwhile, he adds to his reputation as an oddball by collecting fingerprints of townsfolk on glass slides.

The central character in *Pudd'nhead Wilson* is actually someone else—a slave named Roxy, who has a baby son on the same day that her white mistress has a son. The mistress soon dies, leaving Roxy to raise both boys herself. Like the older Prince Edward and Tom Canty in *The Prince and the Pauper*, the two unrelated babies look almost exactly alike. When Roxy becomes afraid of what might happen to her son if he grows up as a slave, she switches the babies. The rightful son of her master thus becomes a slave, and her own son becomes a master.

Roxy gets away with this switch because she is only one part black and 15 parts white, and her son is only ¹/₃₂ black. For more than 20 years, no one but Roxy knows about the switch, until David Wilson reveals the truth in a sensational murder trial. The trial proves that he is no fool, and he makes his case by using the fingerprint evidence he has spent years collecting. The story makes a mockery of the idea that human races are fundamentally different and attacks the institution of slavery. The novel is also one of the earliest to use fingerprint evidence as part of a murder mystery.

Sam also wrote two short novels about Tom Sawyer and Huckleberry Finn. *Tom Sawyer Abroad* is about an aerial voyage across North Africa that Tom, Huck, and the former slave Jim take on a marvelous balloon craft built by a mad inventor. In *Tom Sawyer, Detective*, Tom and Huck go back down the Mississippi River to visit Tom's Aunt Sally and Uncle Silas, whom Sam had introduced in *Adventures of Huckleberry Finn*. Uncle Silas is accused of murder, and Tom comes to his defense in a sensational trial much like the one at the end of *Pudd'nhead Wilson*. It's a story that Tom Sawyer fans are sure to enjoy.

Match Fingerprints

Little was known about using fingerprints to identify people until 1892, when Francis Galton published a book on the subject. *Pudd'n-head Wilson* was one of the first novels to use fingerprint identification as a plot device. In the trial scene that ends the book, David Wilson amazes everyone with a simple demonstration. While he looks in another direction, four people leave their fingerprints on a window pane. Wilson then identifies which person has made each set of marks, drawing on his familiarity with the fingerprints in his collection. You can do the same thing.

WHAT YOU NEED
❋ Clean window panes
❋ Felt-tipped pen with water-based ink
❋ Magnifying glass

Gather several friends together near the window. Use the pen to write each person's name or initials in a list on the window glass, leaving plenty of room by each name. Next to that list, write a list of numbers. Have everyone run their thumbs through their hair and carefully press their thumbs on the glass next to their names. This should leave visible prints. (If you have trouble seeing the prints, look at the glass from a different angle.)

Instruct each person to choose a number from the list on the window while you go out of the room. Ask them each to make new thumbprints next to the numbers they choose while you are gone. Leave the room until they have finished.

When you return to the room, use a magnifying glass to compare the thumbprints next to the two lists, and see if you can match the numbers with the names. Fingerprints look like tiny maps, no two of which are exactly the same. With a little care, you should be able to match all the prints perfectly.

☞ **Wilson studies his fingerprint records.**

Be a Detective

During Uncle Silas's murder trial at the end of *Tom Sawyer, Detective*, Tom gives testimony that unmasks the true murderers, who are sitting in the courtroom in front of everyone's eyes. Using nothing more than his keen powers of observation, he proves that one of these men, whom everyone thinks is deaf and dumb, is the actually the man who was supposed to have been murdered—Jubiter Dunlap. The true murder victim, he explains, is Jubiter's identical twin brother, Jake, who had long ago disappeared.

How does Tom know that the disguised man is Jubiter? By watching him closely during the trial and noticing that when he fidgets, he traces little crosses on his cheek with his left hand. Tom had seen Jubiter do the same unusual thing a year earlier. Many people have similar nervous habits. Sam was a great observer of details, and this is exactly the sort of tiny detail that he loved to notice. In *The Prince and the Pauper,* Tom Canty's mother recognizes him after he becomes king because of a certain way that he jerks his hand in front of his face when he is startled.

WHAT YOU NEED
* Pencil or pen
* Notebook

The ideal location for this activity is a classroom or other place in which the same people regularly sit still for long periods of time. Without letting yourself be noticed, keep a close eye on the other people to see if any of them has a little mannerism similar to that of Jubiter Dunlap or Tom Canty. When you observe such a mannerism, write down the date, the place, and the person's initials, and describe it. Try to watch the same people over a period of several days and add to your notes details of any repetitions or of changes in each person's mannerism.

After you do this successfully several times, you'll find that your powers of observation will have improved.

Joan of Arc

SAM'S LONGEST NOVEL during the 1890s was about the French national heroine Joan of Arc, who led armies against English invaders in the 14th century. Sam had admired Joan throughout most of his life, and he wrote *Personal Recollections of Joan of Arc* to pay tribute to her. He wrote the book in the form of a first-person memoir given by an elderly man who had grown up with Joan and served with her against the English. When Sam described the teenage Joan, he may have been thinking of his own favorite daughter, Susy.

Sam was afraid that if he published the book under the name Mark Twain, people might think it was some kind of joke because he was so famous for his funny books. When the story was first published in *Harper's Magazine,* the name of its author wasn't mentioned. Still, it didn't take the public long to figure out who had written it.

In early 1895 Sam celebrated his 25th wedding anniversary by giving Livy a small French coin as a token of their new poverty. They were not only broke; they also owed a great deal of money to people who had invested in Sam's publishing company and in the Paige typesetting machine. Henry Rogers negotiated a deal that would have allowed Sam to pay off his creditors at 50 cents on the dollar. However, Sam and Livy complained that the deal wasn't good enough: They would only be satisfied if they paid 100 cents on the dollar. The only way Sam could do that was by hitting the lecture circuit again.

 **Susy during her college days.**

Working His Way Out of Bankruptcy

SAM SET A GOAL OF paying off his debts in five years. To accomplish that, he decided to lecture on a grand scale: he would conduct an around-the-world tour! The tour began in London, and it eventually took him across the northern United States and southern Canada to the Pacific Ocean, then to Australia and New Zealand and across the Indian Ocean to Ceylon, India, Mauritius, and South Africa, and ended back in England. Sam would later describe the entire trip in *Following the Equator*, which he wrote after he returned to London. Meanwhile, most of the money from the tour went directly to Henry Rogers, who used it to make payments to Sam's creditors.

In May the family returned to the United States after a four-year absence. Instead of going back to Hartford, they spent two months in Elmira. While the family was there, Sam took care of several business matters, including a new agreement with Harper and Brothers that made that company his exclusive American book publisher. In mid-July he, Livy, and Clara took a train to Cleveland, Ohio, where Sam delivered the first of what were to be 140 lectures. It would be an exhausting trip. Susy and Jean chose to stay in

Elmira. They were to rejoin the family in London the following year.

From Cleveland, Sam went up through Michigan and Minnesota, into Manitoba, and then across the continent, through North Dakota, Montana, Idaho, and Washington, with a stop in Oregon. Sam gave his last North American lecture in Victoria, British Columbia, then he, Livy, and Clara boarded the steamship *Warrimoo* in Vancouver and sailed to Hawaii. Sam had a lecture scheduled in Honolulu, but when the ship anchored there, no one could go ashore because of an epidemic of the highly contagious disease cholera. Sam was horribly disappointed. He had fond memories of the islands and had long dreamed of visiting them again.

The *Warrimoo* then headed to Australia, making a brief stop at Fiji along the way. In mid-September it reached Sydney, Australia. Over the next three-and-a-half months, Sam divided his time between Australia and New Zealand, both of which he found fascinating. He especially enjoyed Australia—which he made the subject of more than a quarter of *Following the Equator*. At the time of his visit there, Australia was made up of seven separate British colonies, including the island of Tasmania. Sam visited all but two of them.

☛ **Sam relaxes on the *Warrimoo*.**

Sam was always fascinated by odd things, and he found plenty of them in Australia. Although Australia was nearly the same size as the United States, it had few people. Its vast wilderness areas must have reminded Sam of the early western frontier of the United States. He enjoyed hearing stories about the country's wild history, its unusual animals, such as kangaroos, and the incredible tracking powers of its aboriginal people. Australia was just the sort of country that Sam loved. To make the trip even more pleasurable, large and appreciative audiences attended all his lectures.

On New Year's Day in 1896 the Clemenses left Adelaide, Australia, for Ceylon (now Sri Lanka), where Sam began an even more fascinating leg of his long journey. He considered Ceylon the first "utterly Oriental" place he had ever visited. Sam spent more than two months crisscrossing India, giving lectures and sightseeing. The whole experience was unlike anything he had ever done before. He explored the cities, studied the ancient temples, rode elephants, and even took a train part way up the Himalayan Mountains.

Apart from Sam's travels in the Holy Land and North Africa in 1867, India was his first exposure to an Asian culture that had almost no ties to European culture. Almost everything about India and Ceylon seemed magnificently alien and fascinating to him: the colorful ways

Australian Trains

DURING THE DAYS of Mark Twain's travels through Australia, the country's two most important colonies used different widths, or "gauges," for their railroad tracks. Since the tracks in New South Wales were narrow gauge and those in Victoria were wide gauge, completely different trains were needed in each territory. As a result, when passengers rode a train from Sydney to Melbourne, they often had to tumble out of bed in the middle of a cold night, walk across the border, and get on another train. Mark Twain called this crazy system "the oddest thing, the strangest thing, the most baffling and unaccountable marvel" the country could show.

☛ **Changing trains in Australia.**

people dressed, the strange buildings, the exotic food, the people riding elephants, the unimaginable crowding in the great cities, and, most especially, the local religions.

🐾 **Climbing the Himalayas.**

🐾 **Excitement in an Indian city.**

From India, the Clemenses sailed to South Africa. Sam turned 60 during this trip, and he was starting to feel his age. The rigors of constant travel and several minor health problems were wearing him down, and he was grateful for the chance to spend two weeks resting on Mauritius—the Indian Ocean island on which

the giant dodo bird had become extinct two centuries earlier.

The family finally reached Durban, on the east coast of South Africa, in May. Sam then spent almost as much time in South Africa as he had in Australia and India, and he found it as fascinating as those other lands. He happened to arrive at an interesting moment. The region's Afrikaner republics and British colonies were at each other's throats. A few years later, the whole region would be caught up in the South African War.

In July Sam boarded a steamship in Cape Town and headed back to England with Livy and Clara. He considered his around-the-world tour completed when he reached London. He then rented a house in nearby Guildford, where the family waited for Susy and Jean to join them from America. After a few weeks, however, they received a disturbing letter reporting that Susy was not well. During a visit with friends in Hartford, she had fallen ill with spinal meningitis, a usually fatal bacterial disease. Livy and Clara sailed for New York the day after they received the news.

On August 18, 1896, Sam was alone in his dining room in Guildford when someone handed him a telegram. Not thinking of anything in particular, he took the message and read: "Susy was peacefully released to-day."

The terrible news that his daughter Susy was dead shocked him, perhaps more so than any other blow he'd received in his entire life. Later, he wrote, "It is one of the mysteries of our nature that a man, all unprepared, can receive a thunder-stroke like that and live."

Of all Sam's children, Susy was clearly his favorite. Neither Sam nor Livy ever got over her death. Sam fell into a depression that made it difficult for him to write anything humorous again. Susy had died in the family's Hartford home, where she had gone after falling ill. She had friends and relatives with her when she passed away, but the fact that she had died inside the house made the idea of the family's returning there unthinkable to Livy. Sam later revisited the house, but Livy never again went near it.

Living in Europe

AFTER SUSY WAS BURIED in Elmira, Livy, Clara, and Jean rejoined Sam in England. It was a sad year for the whole family. They didn't celebrate Thanksgiving or Christmas. Sam tried to lose himself in his writing. In May he finished *Following the Equator*, sent it off to his publishers in New York and London, and then turned to ambitious new writing projects, most of which he never finished.

What Became of the Family's Hartford House

THE CLEMENS FAMILY'S Hartford house sat vacant until 1903, when it was sold to another family. Fourteen years later the new owners rented the house out to a school for boys. After the school moved in 1922, the house was resold. It was later used as a warehouse, and still later was converted to a public library downstairs and a rooming house upstairs. Eventually, a civic organization purchased the house and restored it. It is now open to the public, and visitors can see the house and its furnishings almost exactly as they were in the Clemenses' time.

The manuscripts on which Sam worked during his last years include several long, sad stories about men who are unsure which is real—their nightmares or their waking lives. He also started several stories about an angel with remarkable powers who visits the earth. One of these stories was later published as *No. 44, The Mysterious Stranger*. The story is set in an Austrian printshop in 1490.

Following the Equator was published at the end of 1897 and was an immediate success. Within a few months, Henry Rogers reported to Sam that all his debts had been paid. Sam had aimed to get out of debt within five years, but did it in less than three years—before he had even returned home. The achievement was gratifying, and it was also proof of his

☞ **Outside London, around 1900.**

worldwide popularity. James Pond, his American lecture agent, wanted him to capitalize on this success. He offered Sam the unheard-of sum of $50,000 to deliver 125 more lectures in America. But Sam had finally had it with lecturing, and he turned down the tempting offer.

In the summer of 1897 the Clemens family went to Weggis, Switzerland, for several months and then settled in Austria, where they stayed in and near Vienna for nearly two years. Afterward, they returned to London and lived there until October 1900. The family had no clear reason for making all of these moves. However, through these years Sam's writing kept him busy, and he started to appear in public more frequently. Although he was through with lecturing for money, he gave many speeches—usually at banquets and on special occasions. Everywhere he went, he was recognized and drew large crowds. People were always eager to hear him speak, and he was still able to draw laughs.

By the time the family returned to the United States, Sam had been outside the country for more than five years without a break. He and Livy were both tired and ready to go home. The question now was *where* their home was to be. Their first stop was New York City, where they rented a house on West Tenth Street. Later they lived in a house in Riverdale-on-the-Hudson, which is now part of New York's Bronx borough.

Reports of Mark Twain's Death

WHILE MARK TWAIN WAS LIVING IN London in 1897, a distant cousin of his named James Ross Clemens also happened to be there. When word got out that the cousin was desperately ill, some people thought it was Sam Clemens who was sick, and they even thought that he may have died. A newspaper reporter went to Sam's house to find out if he was dead and was surprised when Sam opened the door to him and appeared to be in good health. The reporter explained his mission and said that he didn't know what to tell his newspaper. Sam suggested that the reporter simply say that the report of his death was "exaggerated."

This story has been told and retold so many times that it seems like it may have been a joke, but the incident really happened.

Triumphant Homecoming

WHEN THE CLEMENSES' ship landed in New York Harbor on October 15, 1900, Sam was greeted like a conquering hero. The story of his bankruptcy was well known, as was his insistence on paying off his debts in full. His success in doing that at his age seemed like a miracle to many people, and it increased the public's already great admiration

☛ **Wearing his University of Missouri robes.**

☛ **Sam and his boyhood friend John Briggs look over the river during Sam's last visit to Hannibal.**

of him. Everywhere he went he met reporters who were anxious to write down every word he said. Before he had left the country, he had merely been the most popular *writer* in America. When he returned, he may well have been the most popular *person* in America.

Knowing that anything he said would be noticed by millions of people, Sam used his fame to write about and comment on many

Smile for the Camera!

Although Mark Twain was one of the world's most frequently photographed people during the 19th century, it is almost impossible to find a photo in which he is smiling. In fact, if you study any 19th-century photos of people, you'll rarely see a smiling face. This isn't because people were less happy

in those days, but because posing for a picture took a long, long time. Modern camera shutters open and close in the blink of an eye. However, in Mark Twain's time, particularly when he was young, cameras were much different. Film took so long to expose that camera shutters had to stay open for minutes at a time. Not only did the cameras have to be held rigidly still, so did the people posing for the pictures. Even slight movements would cause blurs. In the earliest days of photography, people who posed for studio photographs often sat with their heads held in place by metal clamps, which were hidden behind them. Who could smile while doing that?

By the end of the 19th century, camera shutters were getting faster, but even then, people still had to hold their poses for several seconds. The picture at the left, of Mark Twain in front of his former Hannibal home, was taken in 1902. In the lower right corner of the photo is the blur of a young girl who was walking into the picture as the camera's shutter was open. The amount of blurring shows that the shutter was open for several seconds, during which time Mark Twain—who is not blurry in the photo—was standing rigidly still.

How would you have fared as a 19th-century photographer's subject?

WHAT YOU NEED

* Chair
* Mirror
* Stopwatch or timepiece that shows seconds

Set a chair in front of a mirror, and pose as you would if you were having your picture taken in a studio. Have a friend time your pose and watch to see if you move. Hold your pose rigidly for a full minute. You may blink, but you cannot move your head in any direction, wiggle your nose, move your lips or eyes, scratch, sneeze, or cough. To detect whether you're moving, look directly into the mirror at a spot behind your reflection that appears to be close to the edge of your head. Watch to make sure the distance between your head and that spot doesn't change.

Take turns posing with a friend. Try holding a pose with a broad smile. You'll quickly understand why people in old photographs look so serious.

important issues. For example, he was concerned about indications that the United States was becoming an imperial power, like the nations of Western Europe, and he opposed American occupation of the Philippines. He also spoke out against the brutal regime of King Leopold of Belgium in Central Africa's Congo Free State.

In 1902 Sam received an invitation to come to Springfield, Missouri, to receive an honorary doctor-of-laws degree from the University of Missouri. This gave Sam one final chance to revisit Missouri. On his way to the university, he made a surprise visit to Hannibal, where he saw old friends for the last time. Afterward, while passing through St. Louis, he even had one final chance to steer a steamboat—a small harbor craft that was renamed the *Mark Twain* in his honor.

Family Troubles

UNFORTUNATELY, Livy's health began to decline during this period, and that cast a gloom over everything. Sam and Livy were on the verge of buying a house in Tarrytown, just north of New York City, that was to be their first permanent home in a dozen years, when Livy's health took a sudden dive. Instead of settling in Tarrytown, the family spent the summer in York Harbor, Maine. The following year, doctors recommended that Livy be taken to a warmer climate. Sam and Livy decided to go to Florence, Italy, where they had spent a happy year a decade earlier. The family enjoyed their last summer together in Elmira, then left for Italy by ship in late October 1903.

☞ **Sam inspects his old Quarry Farm study during his last visit to Elmira.**

"Adventuring" with Helen Keller

Sam with Helen in 1902, when Helen was 22.

One of Sam's favorite people late in his life was Helen Keller (1880–1968), a young Alabama woman whom he called "the most marvelous person of her sex that has existed on this earth since Joan of Arc." What made Helen extraordinary was that, even though she had completely lost both her hearing and her sight when she was less than two years old, she went on to graduate from college with honors and become a world-famous author. At Sam's own suggestion, the industrialist Henry H. Rogers paid Helen's expenses at Radcliffe College.

Sam first met Helen when she was only 14 and was charmed by her intelligence and her lively sense of humor. He was also amazed that she could recognize a person she may have met only once by the mere touch of the person's finger. Knowing Helen increased Sam's awareness of the special problems of the blind. He thought that being blind would be an "adventure," and he enjoyed telling a story about a time when he had spent two hours groping around "blind" in a giant, pitch-black room, trying to find the exit.

WHAT YOU NEED

* Cloth big enough to serve as a blindfold

This exercise will give you some understanding of what it is like to be without vision. The best place to start is in a familiar room in your home. With the help of a parent or friend—who should remain in the room to keep an eye on you—tie a blindfold around your head to cover your eyes completely. Try to find you way around the room. Do things you regularly do, such as going to the bathroom to wash your hands, going to your bedroom to gather some clothes for dressing for the day, and going to the mailbox to collect the mail. (Make sure that your parent or friend stays close to you to avoid accidents, especially if you go outside.)

To begin to understand what life was like for Helen Keller, imagine that your blindfold will *never* come off. Then, imagine that you cannot hear, either!

Sam rented a large villa outside Florence, and the family settled there, hoping that the warmer weather would improve Livy's health. Sadly, it did not. Livy died peacefully the following June. Although he was devastated, Sam was relieved that Livy's suffering was over. He returned to New York with Clara and Jean, and Livy was buried in the family plot at Elmira.

Over the next several years, Sam lived on Manhattan's Fifth Avenue and busied himself with his writing. He continued working on long stories that he would never finish but also published several small books, including imaginary diaries of Adam and Eve. His daughter Jean's strong opposition to medical experiments on animals moved him to write *A Dog's Tale*. The dog who narrates this story saves her owners' baby from a burning crib, but when her master sees her dragging the baby through a hallway, he beats her cruelly. Later the dog's heroic deed is understood, and the family treats her royally. However, the story ends with the master killing the dog's baby puppy in a scientific experiment, oblivious to the injustice of what he is doing. Sam also wrote *A Horse's Tale*, a story about a wonderful horse that ends up being killed in a bullfight in Spain.

Although Sam had vowed never again to lecture for money, he still enjoyed public speaking. Right up to the end of his life, he was constantly asked to speak at meetings and banquets. He rarely failed to convulse his audiences in laughter, even while he was delivering serious messages on important subjects.

These years were also full of honors for Sam. In 1905 *Harper's Magazine* held a banquet at Delmonico's Restaurant in New York City to celebrate his 70th birthday. It was a great occasion. More than 160 literary figures, business leaders, and friends attended. Before that distinguished audience, Sam recalled his

Sam's table at the Delmonico's banquet.

The famous white suit.

humble first-birthday celebration in Missouri and explained how he had reached his present mighty age:

> → *I have achieved my seventy years in the usual way: by sticking strictly to a scheme of life which would kill anybody else. It sounds like an exaggeration, but that is really the common rule for attaining to old age.* ←

Sam then went on to talk about differences among people's personal habits. For example, he said that he had "never taken any exercise, except sleeping and resting, and I never intend to take any. Exercise is loathsome."

Sam always liked to discuss copyright law during those years. He wanted authors' copyrights to last much longer than they did at the time and also wanted better international copyright protection. He even went to Washington, D.C., and addressed Congress on this issue. During a wintertime visit there, he wore one of the white suits for which he would become famous. In those days, when men dressed formally, they usually wore black suits, especially during the winter months. Sam hated drab clothes, however, especially black suits. In December of 1906, when he testified on copyright before a Senate committee, he startled everyone by appearing in a dazzling white linen suit. It was a sure way to attract attention, and he always loved being the center of attention.

The Last Foreign Travels

SAM BEGAN THE NEXT YEAR by making the return trip to Bermuda with Joe Twichell that they had planned many years earlier. A few months later came news of the most cherished honor that Sam would ever receive in his lifetime: an invitation to come to England to accept an honorary degree from Oxford University. Sam had earlier said that he would never cross the ocean again. However, for an Oxford degree, he would have happily sailed around the world. He left for England aboard the SS *Minneapolis* on June 8, 1907—40 years to the day after he had begun his first transatlantic voyage on the *Quaker City*.

Sam's last visit to England was his most triumphant of all. Everyone, it seemed, wanted to see and hear him. He gave speeches almost every day he was there. King Edward VII even held a garden party in his honor. Sam's visit

Copyright

A COPYRIGHT IS A LEGAL RIGHT that protects authors' writings from being published and sold by other people without permission. (Information on a book's copyright is usually printed on the back side of its title page.) In Mark Twain's time, copyright on a book lasted for 28 years and could be renewed once, giving a total of 56 years of protection. *The Adventures of Tom Sawyer*, for example, was first copyrighted in 1876, so its protection ended in 1932. Consequently, many publishers released their own, unauthorized editions of the book the very next year. Mark Twain would have been pleased to know that Congress finally began extending copyright protection in the late 20th century. In 1998, Congress extended protection to authors to cover their entire lifetimes plus 70 years. If that law had existed in Mark Twain's time, *all* of his books would have been protected by copyright until 1980.

was made all the more fun by an unrelated incident. Shortly before his arrival, the trophy cup of the famous Ascot horse races was stolen. Its disappearance and Mark Twain's visit were both big news stories, and posters advertising daily newspapers featured these headlines together:

→ *Mark Twain Arrives*
  Ascot Cup Stolen ←

☛ **At King Edward's garden party.**

Everywhere Sam went, he jokingly made a point of denying that he had stolen the Ascot Cup. Nevertheless, when the day came for him to march down the center aisle of a great Oxford hall to receive his honorary degree, students cheered wildly and shouted, "Where is our Ascot Cup?" Finally, the chancellor of the university awarded Sam his degree, saying (in Latin), "Most amiable and charming sir, you shake the sides of the whole world with your merriment."

Sam was in distinguished company that day. Among his fellow degree recipients were novelist Rudyard Kipling, sculptor Auguste Rodin, and composer Camille Saint-Saëns. Sam was so thrilled with the academic robe he brought home from Oxford that he looked for every excuse he could find to wear it.

During those years, Sam spent two of his summers in southwestern New Hampshire but afterward decided he wanted a summer place of his own. By this time he was meeting regularly with a young writer named Albert Bigelow Paine, who had won his approval to write his biography. On Paine's advice, Sam bought 248 acres outside Redding, Connecticut, 50 miles northeast of Manhattan.

Stormfield

WITH THE HELP of his daughter Clara and his secretary, Isabel Lyon, Sam arranged to have a house built on his new property. The architect he hired to design it was John Mead Howells, the son of his close friend William Dean Howells. Sam paid little attention to the house's planning and construction. After issuing his general instructions, he said that he didn't even want to see the place until it was ready for him to move into—with a cat purring contentedly by the fireplace.

When the house was finally ready in June 1908, almost everyone in Redding came out to the train station to meet Sam and escort him

☛ **Dictating his autobiography to his secretary and Albert Bigelow Paine.**

Entertaining Angelfish at Stormfield.

to his new home. Sam had planned to live in the house only during the summertime, but it was so comfortable and inviting that he decided to stay there year-round. Built in the style of an Italian villa, the two-story house had 18 rooms and fine views. The property even had two streams with fish. After Sam had been there for a while, he decided to call his new home "Stormfield," after what proved to be the last book of his published during his lifetime: *Extract from Captain Stormfield's Visit to Heaven*. The money he earned from that little book had helped pay for the house.

During the two years he spent at Stormfield, Sam occasionally visited people in New York, but he more often entertained visitors at his home. Among his most frequent guests were young girls, whom he called "Angelfish" and made members of his "Aquarium." His own title was "Admiral." These girls included the daughters of friends, as well as children he'd met during his travels. He always loved the company of children, and since he didn't have any grandchildren of his own, the Angelfish served as substitutes. An Angelfish named Dorothy Quick grew up to become an

Write Maxims

During his last years, Sam enjoyed writing maxims. Maxims are brief sayings that express important thoughts in as few words as possible, as in these examples:

→ *What are the proper proportions of a maxim? A minimum of sound to a maximum of sense.* ←

→ *Few things are harder to put up with than the annoyance of a good example.* ←

→ *Let us endeavor so to live that when we come to die even the undertaker will be sorry.* ←

→ *Few of us can stand prosperity. Another man's, I mean.* ←

Sam's favorite maxims offer lessons on personal conduct or make ironic observations about people's behavior. All the chapters in *Pudd'nhead Wilson* and *Following the Equator* open with maxims from "Pudd'nhead Wilson's Calendar."

Write your own maxims in this activity.

WHAT YOU NEED

✳ Pencil or pen
✳ Paper

Write down maxims that express your views on life. A good place in which to record them would be a notebook that you carry to school. As you go through the school day, observe your classmates and teachers, and try to notice things about them that you admire or dislike. Use your observations to compose maxims that express general truths. These samples will help get you started:

→ *The wise teacher never calls first on the student most likely to have the answer.* ←

→ *The best-liked people in school are those who care least about their own popularity.* ←

April 1. This is the day upon which we are reminded of what we are on the other three hundred and sixty-four.
—*Pudd'nhead Wilson's Calendar.*

author herself. She wrote a book about her friendship with Mark Twain that was later made into a movie called *Mark Twain and Me.*

When the Clemenses had lived in Europe during the late 1890s, Clara had taken up music and decided she wanted to become a concert singer. While she was training, she met a young Russian pianist named Ossip Gabrilowitsch, with whom she fell in love. In October 1909 Clara and Ossip were married at Stormfield. Sam's old friend Joe Twichell performed the ceremony, and Sam wore his Oxford robe. Afterward, Clara and Ossip left for Europe.

In December Sam went to Bermuda with Albert Bigelow Paine, returning in time for Christmas, for which Jean had been making preparations. Sadly, on Christmas Eve, Jean had a heart attack and died while taking a bath. Her health had been shaky ever since the mid-1890s, when she started having epileptic seizures. Nevertheless, her sudden death was one final, terrible shock to Sam. Her body was taken to Elmira for burial, but Sam's own health was too poor for him to make the trip.

Now 74 years old, Sam was almost completely alone in the world. His wife and three of his children were dead, and his sole remaining daughter, Clara, was living across the Atlantic Ocean. In January he made his last

☛ Sam, Jervis Langdon, Jean, Ossip, Clara, and Joe Twichell at Clara's wedding party.

☛ Jean.

journey—a final trip to Bermuda, where he rested and reflected on his long life. When Albert Bigelow Paine learned that Sam's health was failing, he went to Bermuda and brought him home. Shortly after Sam got back to Stormfield, Clara and Ossip arrived from Europe. Four days later, as the sun was setting on April 21, 1910, Sam quietly died.

The next day, Sam's body was dressed in a white suit and taken to New York City, where a large funeral procession and memorial service were held. On April 24 a second service was held in Elmira, and Sam rejoined his wife and children at Woodlawn Cemetery during a driving rainstorm. He had come a long way from his humble beginning in Florida, Missouri.

Resources

Mark Twain's Books

THIS IS A LISTING of Mark Twain's most important books, with comments on their suitability for young readers. All these books are still in print, and the most popular of them are available in many different editions. Whichever titles you choose to read, try to find copies that contain all of the stories' original illustrations. The best editions are those of the University of California Press, the "Oxford Mark Twain" of Oxford University Press, and the Modern Library. If you select other editions, be sure that the copies you read are in Mark Twain's own words—that they are not "abridged," "revised," "rewritten," "adapted," "retold," "modernized," or otherwise changed to suit someone else's idea of what you should read.

The Innocents Abroad (1869). This lively account of Mark Twain's travels in Europe and the Holy Land is a book best enjoyed by older readers who already have some familiarity with European history and the Bible.

Roughing It (1872). This account of Mark Twain's experiences in the Far West is filled with fascinating characters and exciting stories. Readers might enjoy it when they are young, but most will enjoy it more when they are older.

The Gilded Age (1873). Younger readers might enjoy the first 11 chapters of this book, but the rest of the book may be heavy going. The early chapters are a lively fictionalized history of Sam's own family.

The Adventures of Tom Sawyer (1876). This fabulous adventure story can be enjoyed again and again by people of all ages.

A Tramp Abroad (1880). This is one of Mark Twain's less popular travel books, but it has wonderful sections on the Rhineland and the Alps that older readers will enjoy.

The Prince and the Pauper (1881). This story, set in 16th-century England, is one that children like even more than adults do. It puts its heroes through many adventures, while offering glimpses of real English history.

Life on the Mississippi (1883). This long book has many chapters that young readers may not enjoy as much as adults do. However, its early chapters on Sam's time as a cub steamboat pilot are both thrilling and easy to read.

Chapters 53–56, on Sam's boyhood in Hannibal, are also fun to read.

Adventures of Huckleberry Finn (1884). This is a sequel to *The Adventures of Tom Sawyer*, but it's a very different type of story. Huck narrates the novel, which is filled with humor and adventure. It can be enjoyed by children, but older readers will find deeper meanings in it.

A Connecticut Yankee in King Arthur's Court (1889). This novel, about a 19th-century man thrown back into 6th-century England, is best suited for older readers. However, younger readers who like stories about King Arthur and his knights or time-travel stories might give it a try.

The American Claimant (1892). This brief sequel to *The Gilded Age* is one of Mark Twain's zaniest novels but is best suited for older readers.

Pudd'nhead Wilson (1894). This novel about switched identities, slavery, murder, and the meaning of race is a wonderful book for teenagers to read.

Tom Sawyer Abroad (1894). In this brief novel, Tom, Huck, and Jim become accidental passengers on a wonderful balloon craft that carries them to North Africa. It cannot compare with *The Adventures of Tom Sawyer* but is still fun to read at any age.

Tom Sawyer, Detective (1896). This equally short novel is a better story than *Tom Sawyer Abroad*, with which it is often published in a single volume. While visiting Tom's relatives in Arkansas, Tom and Huck get involved in a murder case, and Tom displays his best deductive skills. This story is suitable for readers of all ages.

Personal Recollections of Joan of Arc (1896). This very long novel about France's 14th-century national hero is quite unlike Mark Twain's other books. Older girls might enjoy reading it.

Following the Equator (1897). Mark Twain's account of his travels in Australia, New Zealand, India, and South Africa lacks the humor of his earlier travel books but is full of details about exotic cultures. It is most suitable for adult readers.

Extracts from Adam's Diary (1904) and *Eve's Diary* (1906). Sometimes published together as *The Diaries of Adam and Eve*, these short books are amusing stories about life in the Garden of Eden as it may have been seen by its original residents. Both stories can be enjoyed by readers of all ages.

Extract from Captain Stormfield's Visit to Heaven (1909). This is a delightful story about the wondrous surprises that greet an old seafarer after he arrives in heaven. It is suitable for older children.

No. 44, The Mysterious Stranger (1969). This story wasn't published until nearly 60 years after Mark Twain died. It's not quite finished, but readers won't be left wondering how it ends. It's about an angel with supernatural powers who visits a village in Austria in 1490. The story may be a little dark for younger readers, but teenagers should find it interesting. (Be careful not to confuse this story with *The Mysterious Stranger*, which was first published in 1916 and is still in print. That book has Mark Twain's name on it, but much of it was written by two other men after he died.)

Huck Finn and Tom Sawyer Among the Indians, and Other Unfinished Stories (1989). Nothing in this book was published until long after Mark Twain died. Among its contents are three lively stories in which Tom and Huck are characters. These stories are unfinished but are still fun to read. Harry Potter fans will especially enjoy "Schoolhouse Hill," a story about a magical being who comes to Huck and Tom's village.

Web Sites to Explore

Huge amounts of information on Mark Twain can be found on the Internet. These sites are informative and reliable, and they all have links to other fine sites.

Center for Mark Twain Studies, Elmira College and Quarry Farm
www.elmira.edu/academics/ar_marktwain.shtml
Elmira college offers the best site for exploring Mark Twain's Elmira connections.

Hannibal Courier Post
www.hannibal.net/twain
Mark Twain's hometown newspaper will take you on a tour of Hannibal and connect you to the town's resources on Mark Twain.

Jim Zwick's Mark Twain Site
www.boodocksnet.com/twainwww/
Information on almost everything about Mark Twain that you might want to know.

Kent Rasmussen
http://pages.prodigy.net/arkent
The personal Web site of the author of this book features pictures of Mark Twain unlike any that you will find elsewhere.

Mark Twain Boyhood Home and Museum
www.marktwainmuseum.org
This is another valuable Hannibal-based site.

Mark Twain Forum
www.yorku.ca/twainweb/
Home base of an online discussion group whose resources include recent photographs of important Mark Twain locations (including many photos taken by the author of this book).

A Mark Twain Photo Gallery
www.cmp.ucr.edu/site/exhibitions/twain/
This site features many beautiful photographs of Mark Twain, including some in 3-D. (Be sure to bring red-and-blue glasses!)

Mark Twain Quotes
www.twainquotes.com
A rich collection of Mark Twain quotes, articles, and many other features and illustrations, organized by the noted Mark Twain researcher Barbara Schmidt.

The Mark Twain House, Hartford
www.marktwainhouse.org
The official site of the Clemens family's restored Hartford home.

The Mark Twain Papers
http://library.berkeley.edu/BANC/MTP/
The University of California at Berkeley is home of the largest collection of Mark Twain manuscripts in the world and the place where the finest editions of Mark Twain books are prepared. The Web site has information on project holdings, news, and exhibitions and databases for researchers.

Places to Visit

Berkeley, California. The Bancroft Library of the University of California is the home of the Mark Twain Project, which has the largest collection of Mark Twain manuscripts in the world. Its offices are open only to qualified researchers, but the Project often maintains fascinating exhibitions in the main library's visitor areas.

Elmira, New York. The octagonal study in which Sam did most of his most important writing is open to the public on the campus of Elmira College, which has a major center of Mark Twain studies. Nearby Quarry Farm, where Sam's family spent many summers, is open to the public only for special events. Elmira's Woodlawn Cemetery is the resting place of Sam and all the members of his family.

Hannibal, Missouri. No place brings Mark Twain alive better than this town, in which he grew up. You might enjoy a visit to Sam's restored boyhood home, two fine Mark Twain museums, and the riverfront of the magnificent

Mississippi. If you read *The Adventures of Tom Sawyer* before going there, you'll recognize many landmarks that appear in the novel.

Mark Twain House in Hartford, Connecticut. The Clemens family home has been restored to look as it did in the family's time. The house and nearby center are open to the public almost every day of the year and offer many special programs. Be sure to see the Paige typesetting machine in the basement.

Virginia City, Nevada. The original newspaper building in which Sam worked is long gone, but visitors can still get a feel for what the rowdy mining town and surrounding countryside looked like in his time. The town's Mark Twain Bookshop is filled with memorabilia on both Mark Twain and mining.

Bibliography

☞ *Books especially appropriate for young readers.*

Burns, Ken, Dayton Duncan, and Geoffrey C. Ward. *Mark Twain: An Illustrated Biography.* New York: Alfred A. Knopf, 2001.

Camfield, Gregg. *The Oxford Companion to Mark Twain.* New York: Oxford University Press, 2002.

☞ Clemens, Susy. *Papa: An Intimate Biography of Mark Twain.* Garden City, New York: Doubleday, 1985.

Hearn, Michael, ed. *The Annotated Huckleberry Finn.* Rev. ed. New York: W. W. Norton, 2001.

Kaplan, Justin. *Mark Twain and His World.* New York: Crescent Books, 1974.

☞ Lasky, Kathyrn. *A Brilliant Streak: The Making of Mark Twain.* New York: Harcourt, Brace, 1998.

Leonard, James. S., ed. *Making Mark Twain Work in the Classroom.* Durham, North Carolina: Duke University Press, 1999.

☞ Lyttle, Richard B. *Mark Twain: The Man and His Adventures.* New York: Atheneum, 1994.

☞ McNeer, May. *America's Mark Twain.* Boston: Houghton Mifflin, 1962.

☞ Meltzer, Milton. *Mark Twain Himself.* New York: Thomas Y. Crowell, 1960.

☞ Paine, Albert Bigelow. *A Boys' Life of Mark Twain.* New York: Harper, 1916. (Also published as *The Adventures of Mark Twain.*)

Powers, Ron. *Dangerous Water: A Biography of the Boy Who Became Mark Twain.* New York: Basic Books, 1999.

☞ Quick, Dorothy. *Enchantment: A Little Girl's Friendship with Mark Twain.* Norman, Oklahoma: University of Oklahoma Press, 1961.

Rasmussen, R. Kent. *Mark Twain A to Z.* 2nd ed. New York: Facts On File, 2004.

☞ _____, ed. *Mark Twain's Book for Bad Boys and Girls.* Chicago: Contemporary Books, 1995.

_____, ed. *The Quotable Mark Twain: His Essential Aphorisms, Witticisms, & Concise Opinions.* Chicago: Contemporary Books, 1997.

☞ Skarmeas, Nancy J., ed. *Mark Twain: A Photobiography.* Nashville, Tennessee: Ideals Publications, 1998.

Sloane, David E. E. *Student Companion to Mark Twain.* New York: Greenwood Press, 2001.

Watkins, T. H. *Mark Twain's Mississippi: A Pictorial History of America's Greatest River.* New York: Weathervane Books, 1974.

Welland, Dennis. *The Life and Times of Mark Twain.* New York: Crescent Books, 1991.

Index